Agency, Culture, and Human Personhood

Princeton Theological Monograph Series

K. C. Hanson, Charles M. Collier, and
D. Christopher Spinks, Series Editors

Recent volumes in the series

Lisa E. Dahill
*Reading from the Underside of Selfhood: Bonhoeffer
and Spiritual Formation*

Gale Heide
*System and Story: Narrative Critique
and Construction in Theology*

Michael S. Hogue
*The Tangled Bank: Toward an Ecotheological Ethics
of Responsible Participation*

Philip Ruge-Jones
*Cross in Tensions: Luther's Theology of the Cross
as Theolgico-Social Critique*

Charles Bellinger
The Trinitarian Self: The Key to the Puzzle of Violence

Kevin Twain Lowery
*Salvaging Wesley's Agenda: A New Paradigm
for Wesleyan Virtue Ethics*

Mary Clark Moschella
*Living Devotions: Reflections on Immigration, Identity,
and Religious Imagination*

Gabriel Msoka
*Basic Human Rights and the Humanitarian Crises
in Sub-Saharan Africa: Ethical Reflections*

Trevor Dobbs
*Faith, Theology, and Psychoanalysis: The Life and Thought
of Harry S. Guntrip*

Agency, Culture, and Human Personhood

Pastoral Theology and Intimate Partner Violence

JEANNE M. HOEFT

◆PICKWICK *Publications* • Eugene, Oregon

AGENCY, CULTURE, AND HUMAN PERSONHOOD
Pastoral Theology and Intimate Partner Violence

Princeton Theological Monograph Series 97

Copyright © 2009 Jeanne M. Hoeft. All rights reserved. Except for brief quotations in critical publications or reviews, no part of this book may be reproduced in any manner without prior written permission from the publisher. Write: Permissions, Wipf and Stock Publishers, 199 W. 8th Ave., Suite 3, Eugene, OR 97401.

Pickwick Publications
A Division of Wipf and Stock Publishers
199 W. 8th Ave., Suite 3
Eugene, OR 97401

www.wipfandstock.com

ISBN 13: 978-1-55635-295-9

Cataloging-in-Publication data:

Hoeft, Jeanne M.

   Agency, culture, and human personhood : pastoral theology and intimate partner violence / Jeanne M. Hoeft.

   xiv + 176 p. ; 23 cm. Includes bibliographical references.

   Princeton Theological Monograph Series 97

   ISBN 13: 978-1-55635-295-9

   1. Pastoral theology. 2. Feminist theology. 3. Domestic violence. 4. Wife abuse. 5. Family violence—Religious aspects—Christianity. I. Title. II. Series.

BV4011.3 H64 2009

Manufactured in the U.S.A.

Contents

Preface vii

1 Introduction 1

2 Ontological Interrelatedness 30

3 The Constructed Psyche 63

4 The Constructed Body 97

5 A Pastoral Theology of Human Agency 119

6 A Pastoral Care for Resistance 151

Bibliography 169

Preface

Almost twenty years ago I walked into a battered women's shelter ready to begin a semester internship as part of my seminary education. My studies had somewhat prepared me for the horrendous acts of violence and for the depth of patriarchal injustice that I would encounter there. What I did not foresee on that first day was the courage and resilience of the women I would meet. What I could not have known was that they would inspire me to change my life, to live with more integrity and to make resistance to violence, especially violence against women and children, the center of my work for the following twenty years.

This book was originally written as a dissertation that served as a means by which I could articulate theoretically and theologically some of what I learned from battered women and the people who work with them. Basically I needed a forum for figuring some things out; I needed time to think some things through and make sense of what I and others were experiencing. But it was also my hope that this kind of work could be useful for the church, for the academy, and for those who work tenaciously to end violence against women.

As a dissertation, this manuscript was completed in 2003. I am especially appreciative to Wipf and Stock for publishing this kind of work in a time when many of us who teach and write in the area of pastoral care and pastoral theology are encouraged to write short and simple "how to" books, rather than the theoretical groundings for those same practices.

The method used herein is firmly rooted in the tradition of pastoral theology and its emerging strand of feminist perspectives. Pastoral theology relies on the constructive and analytical movements from practice to theoretical and theological reflection and back to practice. Beginning with the situation of suffering, the "messiness" of human lived experience, pastoral theological construction proceeds to the resources of theology, psychology, and other cognate fields, always with the aim of contributing to a religious community's theological interpretation and returning to the practice of care for human beings. The goal of pastoral theology is to make constructive contributions to theological discourse as well as to impact the practice of care in communities of faith in ways that move toward alleviating human suffering.[1] While this book finds its grounding in the experience of women in violent intimate relationships, it will focus primarily on the movement to theoretical and theological reflection and analysis. Traditionally pastoral theology has, in addition to theology, turned to the field of psychology as a primary resource for understanding human beings. However, in recent years with the influence of postmodernism, pastoral theologians have proceeded to include a cultural analysis in their theological and psychological work. The book will expound on the sources available for use in reflection, given contemporary pastoral theological currents and propose some theoretical and theological constructions.

This work also finds its place in the growing literature of *feminist* pastoral theology, claiming a decidedly political interest toward resisting structures of oppression (intrapsychic and sociocultural) and creating a world that fosters the full flourishing of women.[2] I use a "critical correlational" approach to relating feminist theory, personality theory, and theology in order to propose a theological anthropology appropriate for a feminist pastoral theology.[3] This method correlates questions and propositional answers between fields, noting congruence in foundational assumptions and seeing links between the questions and propositions put forth by one field with those made by another. It also looks for the oppositions and tensions between the fields, assessing what kinds of questions they raise for each other. I also bring to this method

1. Hiltner, *Preface to Pastoral Theology*, argues that pastoral theology is a branch of theology, and therefore concerned with drawing theological conclusions from the perspective of "tender solicitous concern" (see esp. 15–29), but he also seeks a "two-way street" between theology and practice (see 222–23n19).

2. Miller-McLemore, "Feminist Theory in Pastoral Theology," is helpful in distinguishing the work in pastoral theology related to women's issues from work that is explicitly feminist. For some examples of explicitly feminist pastoral theology, see Doehring, *Taking Care*; E. Graham, *Making the Difference*; idem *Transforming Practice*; Miller-McLemore and Gill-Austern, *Feminist and Womanist Pastoral Theology*; Neuger, "Feminist Pastoral Theology and Pastoral Counseling"; idem "Feminist Perspective on Pastoral Counseling with Women"; *Arts of Ministry*; and "Pastoral Counseling as an Art of Personal Political Activism."

3. Doehring, "Method of Feminist Pastoral Theology."

a poststructuralist perspective, which insists that theorizing makes only provisional, contingent, and historicized "truth" claims.[4]

This book proposes that a theological anthropology adequate for a feminist pastoral theology can speak of persons as constituted of and constructed in culture in a manner which retains the value of mind *and* body and also ascribes agency to persons. This thesis arises out of issues raised in the practice of pastoral care for and with victims of intimate partner violence. Although the battered women's movement has been in force for almost thirty years,[5] intimate partner violence continues to be a prevalent problem,[6] and one with which pastors, pastoral counselors, and other pastoral caregivers are continually confronted (whether they are adept at realizing it or not).[7] A growing awareness over the past decade or so in the practice of care for victims and perpetrators of intimate partner violence has raised questions about the intersection of culture and individual suffering, doctrines of God, forgiveness, and sin, and clinical approaches to care.[8] Supported and informed by theories of battered women's syndrome, cycles of abuse, and power and control, many pastoral care providers continue to look for ways to understand and combat the problem of intimate partner violence.[9] My own experience of working with women in this context, listening to their stories and struggles, has suggested that we need to rethink our theories and theologies of what it means to be human in relation to the divine and to

---

4. For a summary of feminist poststructuralist thought, see Butler and Scott, *Feminists Theorize the Political*; and Weedon, *Feminist Practice and Poststructuralist Theory*.

5. Schecter, *Women and Male Violence*.

6. Data on the prevalence of intimate partner violence is difficult to collect given the "private" and often unreported nature of the problem. Estimates of U.S. women who have been abused by their husbands (and this is just one kind of intimate partner violence) range from 30 to 60 percent. See Nason-Clark, *Battered Wife*, 5–7.

7. Nason-Clark, *Battered Wife*, 15, reports that somewhere between 16 and 40 percent of battered women have sought advice from clergy but they report that they were frequently disappointed with the care and response they received.

8. Some of the work in pastoral theology on intimate partner violence includes Adams, *Woman-Battering*; Clarke, *Pastoral Care of Battered Women*; Cooper-White, *Cry of Tamar*; Fortune, *Violence in the Family*.

9. For explanations and background on these theories see Adams, *Woman-Battering*; Cooper-White, *Cry of Tamar*; A. Jones, *Next Time, She'll Be Dead*; L. Walker, *Battered Woman*.

each other, particularly around the issues of body and psyche, cultural construction and agency.

I am suggesting that feminist theories of subjectivity along with process and liberation theologies and an object relations theory of personality can provide the basis for the proposed theological anthropology and thus will provide the sources for the theological and theoretical construction in the book.[10] Empirical process theology, drawing primarily from the work of Bernard Loomer, offers a theological interpretation for a dynamic ontological interrelatedness. Loomer identifies God with the "organic restlessness" of the "web of life" and suggests a direction for describing the ambiguity of life and God.[11] This empirical theological approach values bodily sensibility and material life and offers direction for a theology of human persons as formed of dynamic interrelatedness. Liberation theology adds a theological interpretation of cultural analysis and the workings of power within culture. From a liberation perspective Dorothee Soelle discusses subjectivity in the context of human suffering and elaborates, from a theological perspective, on the power and process of resistance to oppression.[12] The work of W. R. D. Fairbairn and feminist object relations theorists, such as Jessica Benjamin and Jane Flax, offer the base for conceptualizing the process by which a person's psyche develops in the web of relations. Fairbairn's object relations theory of personality development suggests that persons develop through forms of relatedness, internally and externally, which structure the psyche.[13] Benjamin and Flax bring to object relations theory an explicit discussion of cultural prescriptions and involvement in the process of psychological development.[14] From its beginnings, and continuing in its object relations descendants, psychoanalysis, through its theory of

---

10. In addition to points of congruence, these perspectives (process theology, liberation theology, object relations theory, and feminist poststructuralism) also have clear differences in approach and focus. The book will include discussion of these differences and the departures my own argument makes from them. Here I am simply highlighting some aspects of each that I find useful for this project.

11. Loomer, "Size of God."

12. Soelle, *Suffering, Choosing Life, Creative Disobedience*, and Soelle and Cloyes, *Work and to Love*.

13. Fairbairn, *Psychoanalytic Studies of the Personality*; and Scharff and Fairbairn Birtles, eds. *From Instinct to Self*.

14. Benjamin, *Bonds of Love*; idem, *Like Subjects, Love Objects*; Flax, *Thinking Fragments*; idem *Disputed Subjects*.

the unconscious, has provided a theory of the dynamic construction of the psyche and has raised questions regarding our capacity to "choose" our behaviors or to act "freely." It also provides psychological language for seeing the body and psyche as "coincident"[15] and for understanding the internal bases of agency. I turn to feminist poststructuralist theories of subjectivity for more explicit postulations of the mutual constitution of mind/body/culture. Judith Butler serves as a primary resource for a feminist poststructuralist conceptualization of the subject as constituted of and constructed in culture, which also exposes the constructed nature of the categorical distinctions between mind and body. She suggests that that which is presumed to be "natural" (i.e. body) is actually an *effect* of the performative reiteration of norms by cultural regulatory discourses, practices, and institutions.[16] Butler and other feminist theorists[17] also address the issues of agency and resistance in light of women's political struggles and the continuing need to resist oppressive cultural regimes. Butler's formulations, in particular, provide an avenue for addressing the ambiguity of persons, and the power at the root of their formation,[18] as simultaneously victims and agents.

Keeping in mind pastoral theology's concern for practice, after exploring the above theological and theoretical constructions, the book returns to the discussion of care and concern for concrete human suffering in the context of intimate partner violence. This methodological turn can offer a possibility for thinking about the cultural construction of the person in the context of a culture that supports and sustains intimate partner violence. The book will briefly explore the practice of pastoral care from this context given the deep social construction of the person, the indissociability of mind, body, and culture, and the ambiguity at the root of agency, both human and divine.

This book is meant to contribute to the field of pastoral theology in its current concerns for culture and its emerging strand of feminist work.[19] As pointed out above, pastoral theologians are making the

---

15. Butler, *Bodies that Matter*, 59.

16. Butler, *Gender Trouble*; *Bodies That Matter*; and *Psychic Life of Power*.

17. For instance Bordo, *Unbearable Weight*; and Cooey, *Religious Imagination and the Body*.

18. Butler, *Psychic Life of Power*.

19. See Miller-McLemore, "Feminist Theory in Pastoral Theology," 77–94, for a review of feminist work in pastoral theology.

"turn to culture" but have just begun to elaborate on what that means for our understanding of human persons. This book finds its place in the line of work that resonates with Miller-McLemore's call for pastoral theologians to turn to the "living web" of our existence. However, this study also makes a reflexive turn back to the "individual" suggesting that pastoral theology, in the move to cultural analysis, must also offer conceptualizations of how culture makes human persons. Like others in pastoral theology,[20] this work attempts to explicitly address a theological anthropology that understands the human person in the context of culture, and adds to these pastoral theological conversations the poststructuralist perspective that human "beings" are deeply constituted of culture. Although this book will focus on questions about mind/body/culture and agency, and will not offer a comprehensive theological anthropology, it will raise further areas of exploration along those lines.

This book also contributes to the emerging work within pastoral theology of an explicitly *feminist* perspective. Miller-McLemore argues that pastoral theology has been slow to include feminist theory.[21] This project helps that process along. Only a few pastoral theologians have turned to poststructuralism[22] but no one has taken the work of Judith Butler as a primary resource. The contribution also offers some beginning constructions for a feminist poststructuralist pastoral theology. This study also explicitly brings the debates over body and agency that are currently taking place within feminist theory to the field of pastoral theology, where these questions have been touched upon only briefly.[23] The appeals to resistance as a means of individual healing and social change should be supported with a more thoroughgoing analysis of the basis from which resistance occurs.

20. For instance, Graham, *Care of Persons, Care of Worlds*.
21. Miller-McLemore, "Feminist Theory in Pastoral Theology."
22. Bons-Storm, *Incredible Woman*; Doehring, *Taking Care*; and Dunlap, "Discourse Theory and Pastoral Theology" all use poststructuralist theory in their work, although each draws from a different theoretical approach within poststructuralism. I take poststructuralism to include the theoretical perspectives developing from the work of Foucault, Lacan, and Derrida; see Weedon, *Feminist Practice*. Graham, *Making the Difference* and *Transforming Practice*, also takes a poststructuralist approach but uses a broader definition of pastoral theology.
23. In pastoral theology, Dunlap, "Discourse Theory and Pastoral Theology" offers a very brief mention of this question in feminist theory. Graham, *Transforming Practice*, explores it with a little more depth.

While it will not explicitly be written for those in the area of domestic violence, the book does have implications for that field as well, including domestic violence literature within pastoral theology. Although this project will not develop a full-blown analysis of the problem of intimate partner violence, it will respond to current areas of discussion within that field, especially the issue of agency.[24] The work on intimate partner violence within the field of pastoral theology has focused primarily on setting the context of the problem in an oppressive culture and theological tradition, and then looking at the necessary pastoral care responses.[25] This study aims to go one step further and take the experience of women in the context of intimate partner violence and those who care with and for them as the grounds for pastoral theological construction.

I have not made any substantive changes in the dissertation text for this publication. I have, however, revised some of the prose hoping to make it a bit more accessible to the reader. There continues to be a wealth of research and writing in the area of intimate partner violence and yet the issues that I raise in this project are still pertinent to the discussions within that movement/field. In the past few years I have encountered a few activists who are also willing to speak and think critically about the movement's work and yet remain passionately committed to the cause. I have chosen not to update this text with more recent publications on intimate partner violence. Linda Mills's *Insult to Injury* is one of the more thought provoking recent works in the field. Judith Butler's work has continued to grow in popularity among feminist theorists and has several publications beyond what I have referred to here. Though she has not drastically changed her perspective, her newer work might be of interest.

I wish to thank the faculty at the University of Denver and Iliff School of Theology who helped bring this text to fruition as a dissertation, especially my committee chair, Joretta Marshall, committee members, Larry Graham, and Sandra Dixon, Sheila Davaney, who participated in important ways, and Bill Dean who first introduced me to Bernard Loomer and process theology. Two years before the dissertation was completed I began teaching at Saint Paul School of Theology. There I

24. For example M. R. Mahoney, "Victimization or Oppression?"

25. See for instance, Adams, *Woman-Battering*; Cooper-White, *Cry of Tamar*; Fortune, *Violence in the Family*.

received remarkable support and encouragement which enabled a timely completion. I especially want to thank Nancy Howell, who was my first Academic Dean and has been a stimulating conversation partner in process theology, Jim Brandt, who continually finds way to encourage me as a scholar and teacher and whose friendship has been invaluable, and Young Ho Chun with whom I taught in those first years at Saint Paul and whose intellectual voracity and respectful critique were greatly appreciated. Pamela Couture, my first professor in pastoral care and now Academic Dean of Saint Paul, has encouraged me to pursue this publication. She and Joretta Marshall have been exceptional mentors to whom I owe much and by whose wisdom I have been nurtured.

I must also thank the women of Hubbard House, Refuge House, and the National Coalition Against Domestic Violence whose lives and work are at the core of this project. And I must thank the people of Arvada United Methodist Church who were ever understanding of their pastor's school commitments and then pleased to send me off to seminary teaching.

Graduate education is a demanding endeavor at any time, but came for me and my family at a particularly chaotic period in our life together. Everyone made sacrifices; everyone contributed. It is not something that I did, it is something we did. Mary-Margaret, Monica, and Amanda were and are the most immediate relational web of love that unfailingly encourages me toward more life.

Introduction

PASTORS AND OTHER MINISTERS OF CARE SPEND TIME HELPING PERSONS ascertain not only the meanings of and reasons for their suffering, but also the extent to which that suffering can be ameliorated and how to accomplish that amelioration. Persons who are hurting want to know not only why they are hurting but if and how that hurting can be made to stop, or at least lessened. Questions of cause blame, responsibility, and choice are closely tied to questions of what must be done in order for things to get better and who should and is able to do it. Persons come with questions such as: Whose fault is this? How did it get to be this way and what will make it stop? How much of this is my responsibility? What is wrong with me that I have ended up in this kind of situation and what can I do to change things? Or, what do I have to do to make someone else change? On the one hand, things happen to persons that leave them feeling, and often actually, powerless to change their lives and on the other they need a sense of efficacy, and many believe that one's life is what one makes of it. These tensions within persons mirror similar tensions in the broader culture.

On one side of the tension is the realization that in many ways persons' lives are bound by external factors and their position in society, and on the other side is a cultural belief, at least in the United States of America, that any person, however difficult it may be, has the internal capacity to rise above the circumstance of external realities and make life different for oneself if one so chooses. Over the last several decades there has been an increasing awareness of the dynamics of oppression and privilege and the resultant abuses of power in our culture. What could be called "victim movements," social movements based on the claims of victims that they have been excluded, devalued, and abused, have been on the rise. These movements include the Civil Rights Movement, through which African-American persons demand that attention be given to the way racism has structured the world and human thinking, and the women's movement, which similarly forced attention to the sexism that pervades homes, schools, churches, courts, and even psyches. The list can be continued with Native Americans, people with disabilities, and lesbian-gay-bisexual-transgendered persons. External sociocultural realities do limit, often severely, persons lives.

In light of these "victim movements," more consideration has been given to the bias built into language, norms, and perceptions of reality. These movements have heightened sensitivity and changed responses to events such as rape, sexual abuse, domestic violence, hate crimes, and harassment. They are accompanied by a change in perception of what it means to be a person. Much has been learned in the wider culture about how some groups of people have been victimized or treated differently by culture and how that victimization has formed personhood and coerced behavior. It is now more likely that persons are defined by social location and status, as either privileged by or victims of culture. Identity is tied to sociocultural position. Thus we might hear these kinds of statements about who a person is: I am a woman oppressed by a patriarchal culture; I am a black woman in a white world; I am a lesbian in a culture of compulsory heterosexuality; I am a victim and survivor of sexual abuse, domestic violence, or rape in a society where men have power over women's bodies. These messages call attention to the way power structures in culture form identity and act upon persons in order to limit some and encourage others. According to these movements each of us occupies a position of either privileged or oppressed, victim or agent of hegemonic culture. Victims are then called to resist the evils of the culture that oppresses them and the privileged are invoked by their sense of fairness, empathy, guilt, and sometimes fear, to change their ways and perhaps stand in solidarity with the victims.

On the other side of the tension, there seems to be another movement afoot, and this is a movement of choice, of personal responsibility, of self-determination and self-definition. The second movement is what I call the "I can" movement, in which these statements might be heard: I can choose to be who I want to be; I can therapeutically mold, shape and alter my personality; I can control my thoughts, my emotions and my body; I can master my body; I can change the color of my skin, my eyes, my hair, my shape or even my gender; I can be anyone I want to be; I am my own person; I can rise above the circumstances of my life; I refuse to be a victim. These messages that persons are agents of their own lives, that they can create and recreate their worlds, are also rampant in current expressions of cultural values. Although they are most often expressed directed at someone else, "you can," they are taken in as "I should" and "if I don't it is my fault." Success is understood, then, as the result of a person's choices and determination, which, of course, means also that failures are taken to be failures of the same.

Obvious to most is the reality that both of these movements, toward sociocultural limitation and personal responsibility, hold aspects of what we sense to be true and yet we struggle to find ways to hold these aspects of life and personhood together. As one who claims strong feminist convictions and works with victims of abuse, I am particularly concerned with what these tensions mean from the side of the "victim movements." It is a complicated task to set up oneself and one's identity group as victims, deeply harmed by an oppressive culture, who deserve and need the help of others to right the wrongs done *to* them, and, *at the same time,* assert that one and one's peers can act as agents of change, can come together in a political struggle, resist oppression, and change self and the world. If they, or one, have, or has, the power to change the world, then how come they, or she or he, allowed the victimization to happen in the first place? If one can "take charge" of one's life or "reinvent"[1] oneself then who counts as a victim? Where should sympathies lie? How much change can be expected of self and others? Are there *any* "pure" or total victims, who are they and how do they survive?[2]

---

1. A few years ago Oprah made an announcement that the focus of her show would change. The bread and butter of talk shows had been those who could provoke our anger or our pity, the victims and perpetrators of life's more troubling side or of the world's evils. Then Oprah said, "No more. I am not going to promote any more of this feel sorry for ourselves or others. Instead I am only going to do 'positive' shows" (Clemetson, "Oprah at a Crossroads"). Now Oprah focuses on an empowering, uplifting, "take charge of your life" kind of message. The January 2001 issue of her successful magazine, O, expresses this movement perfectly with it's theme "Re-Invent Yourself." The magazine states, "It's what separates winners from whiners" (21).

2. I have set this framework as an arguably oversimplification of movements in popular culture as a way to move into more nuanced theoretical assumptions and questions. I do not mean to suggest that scholars and theoreticians, or the general public, have completely ignored the complexity of the movements and identities. It is beyond the scope of this project to present the full history and development of these cultural events.

Behind these cultural/personal tensions are lurking some rather significant questions about what it means to be a person. To what extent are persons determined by or made of culture and to what extent are they determined by and made of their own choices and actions? As victims and perpetrators, oppressors and oppressed, how able is anyone to resist the prevailing messages of culture? Can we really "re-invent" ourselves? This volume asks the question: How deep does culture go in the construction of human personhood and what are the origins and conditions of the agency needed in order for persons to resist, or change, that culture and themselves? I have found these issues of cultural construction and agency particularly salient in the context of pastoral care with victims of intimate partner violence and it is from that context that this work is forged. I believe that victims of intimate partner violence, and those who care with and for them, have something to offer in the construction of a theological anthropology that can articulate responses to these questions which are in keeping with feminist commitments to social justice. This kind of construction is necessary to help pastors and other ministers of care assist others in resisting injustice and meaningless suffering.

This book develops a pastoral theology of human agency via practice of pastoral care in the context of intimate partner violence, the theoretical work done by those who have studied intimate partner violence, pastoral theological work in the area, and feminist theory. The rest of this chapter explores the ways that the tensions between agency and resistance, victim and agent, become apparent in the fields of intimate partner violence, pastoral theology, and feminist theory. First we explore the development of various perspectives in the field of intimate partner violence and demonstrate some of the concrete ways that the victim/agent tension arises in efforts to stop domestic violence. Next we turn to the move in pastoral theology from individualized psychological understandings to concern for cultural construction and identify the need for a pastoral theological anthropological of agency in light of this turn. Finally in this introductory chapter, we look at the debates in feminist theory over the extent to which a cultural construction of personhood can be useful to a movement that requires agential subjects.

Intimate Partner Violence

The battered women's movement, organized thirty years ago, has worked to raise the public's awareness of domestic violence and to move the focus away from the problems of individual women and toward the problems of culture.[3] According to the battered women's movement, he primary dynamic of intimate partner violence is rooted in patriarchal control of women's bodies and the abuse of power when it is used to maintain control of women. The purpose of battering, the regular use of violence or coercion in intimate relationships, is for one partner to establish control over the other, usually a woman. Ann Jones defines battering as "a process of deliberated intimidation intended to coerce the victim to do the will of the victimizer."[4] The justice system, churches, mental health professions, and economic systems have all contributed to and sustained woman battering. The dynamic of intimate partner violence must be understood in terms of multiple factors. Of particular interest to this project is the intersection of culture, psyche, and body.

Culture, Psyche, and Body

Approaches to theorizing the problem of domestic violence have taken multiple forms and directions over the last few decades. Intimate partner violence has been explored through a wide range of perspectives, including psychological, sociological, cultural, medical and legal. Given the foci of this project on psyche, body, culture, and the means by which these three "make up each other" this section gives a brief representation of domestic violence literature as it addresses these three areas for exploring and comprehending the dynamics of intimate partner violence.

Researchers Richard Gelles and Murray Straus, who did some of the first empirical research on family violence, approach the epidemic of violence in U.S. families in the context of violence in society. Family is the "cradle of violence" in the culture, the place where violence is nurtured and passed on.[5] Families use violence in response to stress and conflict and produce children who then perpetrate violence in an endless intergenerational cycle. Gelles and Strauss suggest that social

---

3. Schecter, *Women and Male Violence*.
4. A. Jones, *Next Time*, 88.
5. Gelles and Straus, *Intimate Violence*.

exchange theory can help explain family violence in terms of rewards and punishments. Family violence continues because the rewards of anger catharsis, effective discipline, control and power outweigh the costs. In short intimate partner violence happens because of a lack of social consequences or, as Straus and Gelles put it, "because it can." Society is violent because families are violent and families are violent because society perpetrates and supports violence.

> Violence in the home, we have found, is not altogether unpredictable or unexpected. In our society, a person's earliest experience with violence comes in the home—spankings and physical punishments from parents. We learn that there is always going to be a certain amount of violence that accompanies intimacy. Moreover, we learn that children 'deserve' to be hit. That 'sparing the rod spoils the child.' We grow to accept violence as a way of solving problems. Violence is also considered an appropriate means of expressing oneself. Violence in the home is not the exception we fear; it is all too often the rule we live by.
>
> Our society concentrates on violence in the streets because our goal is not just to eliminate violence but to enforce some kind of social order that renders the world predictable (and hopefully safe). We ignore violence in the home precisely because it is so predictable and because whatever harm it does cause is traded off against the safety and sanctity of the family.[6]

Intimate partner violence happens because the adults involved grow up in violent homes, not as a deviation from societal norms but as the norm itself. The only difference then, for Gelles and Straus, between spanking and murder is a matter of degree.

Other literature suggests that a closer look at the family in its larger sociocultural context will point to the roots of intimate partner violence in the specific violence of patriarchy.[7] Domestic violence, from this perspective, is a by-product of the social problem of male domination of women, patriarchal ideology and structure. Judith Herman and Lenore Walker, both of whom are primarily focused on the psychologi-

---

6. Ibid., 19–20.

7. Other kinds of family violence such as child abuse have also been linked to patriarchy. See, for instance, Gordon, *Heroes of Their Own Lives*; and Stark and Flitcraft, *Women at Risk*. A discussion of other modes of violence in families is beyond the scope of this project but by this restriction of topic I do not intend to suggest that there are not important links.

cal dynamics and consequences nevertheless root domestic violence, or woman-abuse, in the problem of patriarchy. Walker points out that the problem is "too widespread" to be accounted for in individual pathology and must be considered a "serious social disorder" of a "sexist" society caused by male domination.[8] Herman likens the context of domestic violence to war, "[t]he subordinate condition of women is maintained and enforced by the hidden violence of men. There is war between the sexes. Rape victims, battered women, and sexually abused children are its casualties."[9] Violence against women as an outgrowth of male domination then must also be seen in the larger ideologies and structures of patriarchy, such as, hierarchical orderings of institutions and relationships, definitions of "appropriate" violence, medical models for diagnosis of dysfunction/disease and treatment aimed at individuals, the privatization of family, and related ideals of autonomy, self-sufficiency, obedience to authority, loyalty, and dedication.[10]

Many authors emphasize the development of family ideals within a patriarchal culture, especially the related ideals of marriage and motherhood. For instance Dobash and Dobash point out that our culture's couple oriented society builds into marriage a narrower range of relations with others, especially for wives and mothers, a movement that assists in the isolation that can sustain battering.[11] When the norm of male authority in the home is traced historically through the clash of capitalism and patriarchy, Evan Sark and Ann Flitcraft suggest that woman battering can be linked to tensions over "women's work," the increasing autonomy of women, and the ideological split of public and private.[12]

Ann Jones, grounding her discussion from a criminal justice position in women's "absolute right to be free from bodily harm,"[13] also addresses the culture of patriarchy and its "conflation" of sex and violence. Jones suggests that under patriarchy men get to define events,

---

8. L. Walker, *Battered Woman Syndrome*, 43.

9. Herman, *Trauma and Recovery*, 32.

10. Dobash and Dobash, *Violence against Wives*; Gondolf and Ellen, *Battered Women as Survivors*; A. Jones, *Next Time*.

11. Dobash and Dobash, *Violence against Wives*.

12. Stark and Flitcraft, *Women at Risk* .

13. A. Jones, *Next Time*, 4.

for instance, as either "assault" or "argument," "rape" or "making love."[14] Language itself is a tool of coercion. What is "normal" aggression in sex and what counts as too much is defined by men, as evidenced in debates over pornography. Domestic violence under patriarchy could be defined as a "crime of passion" and the problem as one of "excessive love."[15] Jones reminds us of the many media portrayals of romance as a woman being "carried off," "whisked" away, or "hotly pursued."[16] Women appear to consent but in fact have little power to do so by virtue of their social position and their "psychological conditioning"[17] under patriarchy.

> The point is that as long as a 'certain amount' of sexual and physical 'fighting' is thought natural, civilized, desirable, or necessary in marriage, violence will always be thought to occur with the woman's consent, the woman's provocation, the woman's solicitation, the woman's pleasure, just as rape was once thought to be provoked, solicited, consciously desired, and subconsciously needed by women victims of rape. Battering (which commonly includes marital rape), like stranger rape, is a crime of power and control committed mainly by men against women, a crime in which the perpetrator does not consult the victim's wishes and from which he will not let her escape.[18]

The rationalization of a certain amount of "allowable" or "normal" violence in relationship obfuscates the underlying cultural matrices at work in the practices of not only intimate activity but in language itself. These same dynamics are played out in same sex relationships where, although the gender identities of partners may not be male and female, the paradigm for relationships and violence remains. This is not to say that there are not additional factors and that those factors do not significantly change the experience of persons in relationships but that violence in same sex relationships does not negate the impact of a patriarchal cultural ideology.[19] Cultural values, images, structures of power

---

14. Ibid., 107.
15. Ibid., chap. 4, "Language of Love."
16. Ibid.
17. Ibid., 100.
18. Ibid., 126.
19. For this approach to same sex battering see Lobel, eds., *Naming the Violence*; and Renzetti, *Violent Betrayal*.

and social arrangements function in a myriad of ways to encourage, if not create, and sustain intimate partner violence.

References to learned helplessness, trauma, survival, guilt, anger, jealousy, and powerlessness frame discussions of the psychological dynamics at play in intimate partner violence. A few psychological approaches understand intimate partner violence in terms of the victim's personality disorder. In these approaches battered women are described with a series of disordered characteristics: self-destructive, masochistic, dependent, co-dependent and low self-esteem, which are the conceived as the primary contributing factor to perpetuated violence and thus also the primary focus of "treatment."[20] Most empirical research has not found a basis for such labeling. No personality traits or other characteristics, other than their gender, are shown to predict a likelihood of battering.[21]

Most discussions regarding the victims of intimate partner violence discuss psychological dynamics in terms of the effects of abuse. Psychologist Lenore Walker was interested in the reason women stay in abusive relationships. In addition to the social factors, she also found a syndrome, later called Battered Woman's Syndrome,[22] which could be understood from the social psychological theory of learned helplessness. In essence the theory suggests that over time and escalating violence, victims develop a certain paralysis and passivity, an inability to respond effectively. This syndrome is sustained by a culture that perpetuates the powerlessness of women through sex-role stereotyping. Walker found that both batterers and battered women have feelings of powerlessness and "fear they cannot survive alone."[23] Battered women have "traditionalist" approaches to sex roles, blame themselves for the batterer's actions and believe that she alone will be able to resolve the problem in the relationship. Dobash and Dobash also suggest that a woman's cultural worth as wife and mother and her obligation to the family and domestic sphere increases the sense of responsibility. They suggest that as the violence escalates over time a woman victim expe-

---

20. For instance, Celani, *Illusion of Love*; and Norwood, *Women Who Love Too Much*.
21. A. Jones, *Next Time*, 162–66.
22. Walker, *Battered Woman Syndrome*.
23. Ibid., 43.

riences a "diminishing estimation"[24] of herself and her batterer and a loss of affection for him, though they may remain bound to a marriage. Jones adds further specificity to discussions of blame and responsibility, stating that battered women do indeed blame the batterer for actions of abuse, not themselves, but they do blame themselves for the specific acts that "set him off" and for "sticking around as long as they did."[25] She goes on to say, "Implicit in such remarks, of course, is the desire to be in control of one's own life, the need to believe that one can be safe by not repeating the same 'mistake.'"[26] Battered women hold on to the belief that they can change their lives. Most try to figure out, especially initially, how to change their own behavior in order to help the batterer stop battering.

The interplay of helplessness and resistance, battered women as victims and survivors, has led to many critiques and alternatives to Walker's syndrome theory. Edward Gondolph's study leads him to suggest that battered women would be more aptly described as "survivors," than victims.[27]

> In our research, shelter women do not appear to display the 'victim' characteristics commonly ascribed to those who are battered. They appear instead as 'survivors,' acting assertively and logically in response to the abuse. They contact a variety of 'help sources,' from friends and relatives to social services and the police, but with little result. The deficiencies seem, therefore, to be in the helping sources to which the women appeal and confide.[28]

Gondolph's research shows that in fact as the violence escalates a battered woman's efforts to get help increase, rather than decrease as a theory of passivity or helplessness would indicate, and she is less and less likely to engage in self-blame. He then suggests that we should view battered women as resilient, persistent, and strong, characteristics developed perhaps in their roles of birthing and relational nurturing. The symptoms observed as guilt, depression, and low self-esteem may arise

---

24. Dobash and Dobash, *Violence against Wives*, 126.
25. A. Jones, *Next Time*, 163.
26. Ibid.
27. Gondolf and Fisher, *Battered Women as Survivors*.
28. Ibid., 2.

not from the repeated violence of their partner, whom they continue to resist, but from the violence of an unresponsive and deficient community to whom they have repeatedly turned for help. Their interests in saving the relationship and symptoms of separation anxiety can be interpreted as developing from a sense of failure in their prescribed cultural role and the fear of the unknown as their social status changes.

Herman turns to trauma theory, originally developed to interpret symptoms displayed by war veterans, as a means to comprehend the complex of psychological phenomenon displayed by victims of domestic violence.[29] According to Herman, intimate partner violence is a complex form of trauma that results in symptomatic similarities to post-traumatic stress disorder but complicated by the on-going nature of the trauma as opposed to a discrete traumatic event. It is the character and severity of the event that determines the amount of damage to the victim, not the victim's personality or psychological health. While no two people will respond the same, individual differences of history and constitution shape a variety of responses; everyone has a "breaking point." Repeated trauma such as that of intimate partner violence damages the structure of the self, connection to community, and frameworks of meaning. Over time victims will relinquish all these in the interest of survival and may eventually lose the will to fight, or live and move into extreme passivity. Victims may experience shame, guilt, lack of trust, both desperation for and withdrawal from relationship. Their bodies betray them and remain at a hyper state of arousal and vigilance, ready for the worst; their minds become practiced at altered states of consciousness and deep introspection in order to make what is happening to them more bearable. Identity loses its continuity. These symptoms should be seen, not as "giving up" but rather as strategies for survival.

Given the theological intent of this project and its grounding in an ontological interrelatedness (to be developed later) it is not sufficient to focus solely on the experiences of the victim. How does the literature portray and interpret the psychological dynamics of batterers? Most of the literature agrees that, much like battered women, there are not personality traits or social demographics, except gender, that predispose someone to perpetrate violence against an intimate partner. As Herman points out the "most consistent feature, in both the testimony of victims

---

29. Herman, *Trauma and Recovery*.

and the observations of psychologists, is [the perpetrator's] apparent normality."[30] Some batterers have alcohol problems; some have personality disorders; some have trouble handling anger and stress outside of the home, but many do not. Some batterers display impulsivity and some are more deliberate. Gondolph suggests that there are different types of batterers based on behavioral differences: the sociopathic whose violence is most severe and extends beyond the home, the antisocial who perpetrates less injurious physical abuse with some violence outside the home, the chronic batterer who does not use weapons but commits severe verbal and physical abuse and, like the antisocial, blames the victim for the abuse, and the sporadic batterer who commits physical abuse with much less frequency and minimal physical injury and will often be apologetic after an attack.[31] Batterers present a variety of backgrounds, motivations, and behaviors.

Research has indicated that a high percentage of batterers come from violent childhood homes, in Walker's sample 81 percent.[32] Angela Browne, one of Walker's associates, reports that men who witnessed violence between parents were three times more likely to hit their wives.[33] These statistics indicate that most batterers have childhood family histories of violence but do not indicate that most male children who witness violence in their childhood homes will become batterers. Browne suggests that with these childhood experiences come feelings of guilt, fear, and helplessness that contribute to the batterer's use of violence.

The sense of male entitlement and a belief in the stereotype of male authority is one characteristic that does typify batterers. Perhaps it is this conviction along with the feelings held over from childhood that contribute to the use of coercion to maintain male privilege and the tendency for most to blame others for their violence. Dobash and Dobash describe it this way: "When a husband attacks his wife he is either chastising her for challenging his authority or for failing to live up to his expectations or attempting to discourage future unacceptable behavior."[34] After the attack most batterers fail to show remorse, deny

30. Ibid., 75.
31. Gondolf and Fisher, *Battered Women as Survivors*, 64–67; and further developed in Gondolf, *Batterer Intervention Systems*.
32. Walker, *Battered Woman Syndrome*, 19.
33. Browne, *When Battered Women Kill*, 31.
34. Dobash and Dobash, *Violence against Wives*, 122.

responsibility, and minimize the damage. They believe that they were provoked by a fundamental failure of one who should be attending to their needs. Historian Linda Gordon suggests that "Batterers were not necessarily conscious of their goals. Often they felt so wounded by women's behavior, and so desperately longed for a wife's services, that they experienced their violence as uncontrollable; they felt they had no recourse. Their sense of entitlement was so strong it was experienced as a need."[35] Jones reminds us that abusive men do not think of themselves as "soldiers in the cause of male supremacy" but rather in their minds they are exercising their right to ordinary needs, "dinner on the table, cold beer on call, sex on demand, quiet kids, clean socks."[36] They feel threatened and victimized and need to regain control of their lives and see the victim as an object whose purpose is to fulfill their needs.

The psychological dynamics should not distance us from the material bodily events of intimate partner violence. Domestic violence is a concern for the criminal justice and medical fields precisely because it results in bodily harm. The pattern of coercive behaviors include intimidating looks and gestures, smashing things, harming pets, yelling, stalking, isolation, name calling, playing mind games, controlling access to money and transportation, displaying weapons, and many more. According to Dobash and Dobash, victims are most often slapped, punched, or kicked.[37] They are also assaulted with language and virtually all physical attacks are preceded with verbal assaults. Many are threatened with weapons, acts that will not send them to emergency rooms or doctor's offices but are physically injurious nonetheless. The Power and Control Wheel, a widely used graphic for understanding the many modes of battering, makes it clear that a wide range of behaviors are used but that they all serve the purpose of control over the victim.[38]

The material harm that accompanies intimate partner violence is, of course, not limited to the victim, although the level and kind of harm is significantly different for batterers. Homicide and suicide are very real concerns. Perpetrators are often threatened with arrest or are arrested and may spend time incarcerated. Both victims and perpetrators

---

35. Gordon, *Heroes of Their Own Lives*.
36. A. Jones, *Next Time*, 96.
37. Dobash and Dobash, *Violence against Wives*, 122.
38. The Power and Control Wheel was developed by the Domestic Abuse Intervention Project, 206 Fourth St., Duluth, MN 55806, and is widely available.

must be concerned with the material realties of survival in our world, such as the need for housing, food, work, money, and caring for other dependents. Batterers too are kicked, slapped, pushed, and screamed at.[39] The power of the variety of ways both victims and perpetrators are formed by and must deal with the prejudices and systematic injustices of racism, heterosexism, ageism, and classism also cannot be overlooked.[40] Intimate partner violence is materially carried out. Bodies are used to intimidate and to resist and all bodies involved are harmed.

Questions of Resistance and Agency

The purpose of this book is to explore not the whole realm of dynamics in intimate partner violence, but the specific dynamics of agency and resistance shown by victims. Stephanie Rodriguez, a formerly battered woman, who endured years of torture and abuse from her husband, describes in her autobiography the power to resist and the ambiguities that arise therein.

> For the first time in my life I went against the silly "plan." I ran.
> Beside the refrigerator was a two and a half foot piece of two-by-two....
> A quick "whack" from the two-by-two stopped it, right then. Just like that, it ended. No praying or waiting for a disinterested god to take action. I did it myself with one quick whack.
> Unfortunately, I couldn't muster another. I dropped the board; he picked it up. The rest of the night was pretty messy. It involved emergency people. But a change had begun.
> I grew away from my god. The further I got from him, the closer I got to myself and my family, to reality. The less I depended on him, the more I depended on me. I even decided that paradise could wait, at least until I got my kids grown. They needed me. I was quicker to action on their behalf than was God. I didn't know why.[41]

---

39. This should not be interpreted to mean that these acts are equal to those acts perpetrated by the batterer upon the victim; rather I am simply making the point that this dynamic of coercion involves the bodies of all parties but certainly with different motivations and outcomes.

40. This book does not address issues related to the intersection of intimate partner violence and race, sexual identity, class, etc. For some sources that do address these issues see Eugene and Poling, *Balm for Gilead*; Lobel, ed., *Naming the Violence*; Renzetti, "Challenge to Feminism"; White, *Chain, Chain, Change*.

41. Rodriguez, *Time to Stop Pretending*, 14.

For a moment Rodriguez accessed something that enabled her to act against the prevailing hegemony and to resist the on-going and systematic victimization in which she lived. And yet from that same moment, and others like them, she also speaks of realizing the ambiguities that arise when "the victim" acts like "the monster."

> How are monsters made? I don't know, I don't know, and I don't know.
> Monsters, it turns out, are very complicated things. Seems any one of us might be a monster or a victim, or the creator of a monster or a victim, depending on what day you talk to us.[42]

Rodriguez's description has several implications for a theology of human persons and their care, and illustrates the direction of this work.

One approach to Rodriguez's story, following those few who see battering as a problem of personality and character, could erroneously understand it as the story of a sad and possibly sick woman. Who else would have put up with the kind of abuse she did? The focus of concern for Stephanie in that case would be directed toward her individual psyche and family history. The problem would be framed in terms of codependency, "women who love too much,"[43] or masochism. The questions that a pastor or minister of care might ask would center on why *she* allowed this to happen or what did she do to provoke it, implying that her actions and these events were her choice and self-determination. Even Rodriguez's own words could be used in an attempt to justify this interpretation. She writes:

> I come from a long line of battered women, and like each of them, I grew into my mother's warped sense of identity, confusing vulnerability with femininity. I also mistook crazed and brutal beatings for impassioned, jealous love. I found a man who was every bit as impassioned and jealous as my own father, and settled down to bask in the love. It was all I needed. That and a good healthcare plan.[44]

From a different perspective, one that understands intimate partner violence as a sociocultural problem, Rodriguez's situation would not be considered as her fault, nor would her husband's actions be in-

---

42. Ibid.
43. Norwood, *Women Who Love Too Much*.
44. Rodriguez, *Time to Stop Pretending*, 6.

terpreted as jealousy. His beatings were a way to establish control over her the way society also objectifies and establishes male control over women. Economic dependency, women's role as mothers, commitment to marriage, faith in an omnipotent God and fear for her life, all worked together to batter Rodriguez and keep her in this relationship. Early in its history the battered women's movement established itself as a political resistance movement whose purpose it was to change these sociocultural structures of oppression that contributed to woman battering. Since then heories about the way that power is structured, used and abused in our world have grown in sophistication. In response, shelters have been established, laws changed and many are now familiar with the Power and Control Wheel and the cycles of abuse. Feminists have developed sociocultural explanations of why a woman might stay in a violent relationship and how that question of "why a woman stays" is itself victim-blaming. Patterns of control and the economic and cultural forces that work to constrain women's freedom have been identified. Society and the church are becoming more educated about the greater risks of death that a woman faces if and when she does leave.

But some problems have arisen that highlight the reason for my questions about agency and resistance. For instance, battered woman syndrome, which explains battered women's helplessness, while it provides a seemingly useful defense when a battered woman kills, can also be used against them. As the legal system has become more savvy about battered woman syndrome it works to fine tune a definition of what counts as a "real" battered woman and uses that definition to discredit many victims who show signs of *not* being helpless, for instance, when they fight back or call the police or leave (which is most battered women).[45] An either/or dichotomy is set up with "all-victim" on one side and "all-agent" on the other.[46] Child custody issues arise when it is debated whether or not a victim has been so victimized that she is unable to protect or take care of her children.[47] As Nancy Hirschman points out in her essay on the concept of choice and freedom in relation to battered women, when a woman's wants, as in to return or stay in a violent relationship, are defined as not "really" hers but rather a product

---

45. A. Jones, *Next Time*, 103.
46. M. R. Mahoney, "Victimization or Oppression?"
47. Schneider, "Particularity and Generality."

of patriarchy, she is doubly victimized by being told what is "really" her and "really" not her.[48]

As an explanation for and cause of the victim's actions, culture is used in a way that allows the victim's action, specifically her action of violent resistance, or apparent inaction, to be excused,[49] but when attention is turned toward perpetrators a tension arises. Many argue that cultural oppression, played out in a violent intimate relationship, determines the actions or inactions of the victim, the battered woman, and therefore excuses her or at least severely limits her culpability; but then they do not argued that cultural determination excuses or limits the culpability of the perpetrator.[50] While the batterer's actions are explained in terms of a culture of oppression, and the batterer's identity as an oppressor in that culture, we expect *him* to be *individually* able to resist that culture. In other words he is expected to be able to determine his actions himself, to take "personal responsibility"[51] and thereby stop doing what he has been doing. Sharon Lamb describes the problem in terms of our desire for "pure victims" and "pure perpetrators" so that individual blame and responsibility can be neatly and categorically assigned.[52] It is my contention that while it is legitimate to expect that the batterer, as compared to the victim, is better able to resist the culture that sustains, if not encourages, intimate partner violence, and therefore stop the battering, we need to take a closer look at the assumptions, and their implications, about agency and resistance behind this expectation.

These tensions invite elaboration first of the interconnections between culture and individual person, and second of how those interconnections impact the agency a person needs in order to resist. Resistance, as withstanding or refusing to comply with a prevailing force, assumes agency, which is the capacity or ability to act, to influence or have an effect, and usually understood as "self-determined" action.

---

48. Hirschmann, "Theory and Practice of Freedom."

49. For discussions regarding this issue see M. R. Mahoney, "Victimization or Oppression?"; Renzetti, "Challenge to Feminism"; Schneider, "Particularity and Generality."

50. Lamb, *Trouble with Blame*, also makes this point.

51. Pastoral theologian Pamela Cooper-White, for one, argues this in "An Emperor without Clothes."

52. Lamb, *Trouble with Blame*. These issues are also taken up in Lamb, *New Visions of Victims*.

I try to understand these issues in culture, person and agency by asking, "What enables victims of intimate partner violence to resist? And what do victims of intimate partner violence have to teach us about the construction of human personhood and agency in relation to culture?[53] Responses to these questions will help pastoral caregivers be able to respond more appropriately, not only when working with victims and perpetrators of intimate partner violence, but to anyone trying to ascertain, in the face of meaningless suffering, what must be done and who is able to do it.

In order to retain the feminist contributions and commitments valued by the battered woman's movement, a theory of agency and resistance must do so without trivializing the depth of victimization and cultural oppression of women which is the basis for feminist political struggle. Victims of intimate partner violence offer us complex ways to think about the tensions between agency and victimization and what motivates and sustains acts of resistance.

In preparation for writing her story Rodriguez stated:

> I examined my life, from every possible angle, looking for the secret, the way out. What, I wondered, had made me leave him that day, after all those years? Needless to say, I never figured it out. For me, a certain something had clicked inside me and everything was different. To this day, I don't know why. It had just happened.[54]

I am interested in the moment in which "something clicked." How did it happen? When Rodriguez picked up the two-by-two for a moment she accessed something that enabled her to act against the prevailing rule and to resist the on-going and systematic victimization in which she lived. The resistance seemed to arise "just like that." From where, I ask. What enabled her, and others like her, to resist and how can

---

53. I am choosing to ask this question from the viewpoint of the victim for several reasons. First, it is the victim who is most often the one with whom ministers of pastoral care will have the most contact. Second, pastoral theology has a history of beginning theological construction from the perspective of care for the suffering. Third, taking this viewpoint finds support in liberation theology with its "preferential option of the poor" and in feminist theory with "standpoint epistemology." I am not unaware of the complexities, ambiguities, and issues at stake in this choice and in fact to some extent they fuel the questions raised herein. These issues will be discussed as this thesis develops.

54. Rodriguez, *Time to Stop Pretending*, 8.

we understand her capacity to act against abuse under such devastating victimization? If we could understand more about what enabled her, perhaps that could be translated into fostering that same thing in both victims and perpetrators seeking to resist the violence by which they are victimized or through which they victimize others.

Development of a Pastoral Theological Perspective

Theorizing agency from the context of intimate partner violence is not the only intent of this project. As a work in pastoral theology, the project raises theological questions and proposals, particularly regarding issues of theological anthropology, and aims to make a contribution to the practice of caring response on the part of faith communities. Seward Hiltner defined pastoral theology as a field within practical theology that is focused on events in human life when those events cause suffering and call for theological construction and a pastoral response from the perspective of "tender and solicitous concern" for persons.[55] Pastoral theologians have historically focused on situations of individual (or family) human suffering and the practice of caring response, most often from pastoral care specialists, pastors and pastoral counselors. With the postmodern turn to particularity and cultural context, the parameters of pastoral theological concern are now expanding from the individual to include the "living web" of our human existence.[56] The subject of pastoral theological inquiry is moving from an individually focused psychological approach to consideration of the impact of culture on the life of the individual. No longer can pastoral theologians conceive of the individual outside of her or his social and cultural context.[57] Psychological factors are influenced by and intertwined with economic, political and cultural systems. A person's development is impacted by gender, race, sexual orientation, class and other cultural "realities." What once may have been considered *individual* problems are now being carefully evaluated for their societal and cultural foundation.[58] Pastoral theologians must now also become more explicit in theorizing the indi-

---

55. Hiltner, *Preface to Pastoral Theology*.
56. Miller-McLemore, "The Living Human Web."
57. L. Graham, *Care of Persons*.
58. For an example, see Poling, *Abuse of Power*.

vidual in relation to culture as they form their theological constructions and pastoral responses.

Attention to culture's messages and structures regarding women encouraged the last decade's pastoral theology written by or focused on women's experience. The influence of psychologies of women, such as the work of Carol Gilligan, Nancy Chodorow, and Jean Baker Miller, is apparent in current psychological approaches within pastoral theology, especially, of course, in works specifically focusing on women.[59] These theorists argue that women's psyches develop in a culture that disadvantages women resulting in psychological development that proceeds differently than men's. However, while changing psychological theories have been one result of the shift toward culture, there has also been a turn toward reevaluating the tendency to define women's "problems" in psychological terms when psychological issues may indeed be secondary to the sociocultural devaluation of women. When Rodriguez writes of confusing violence for love and vulnerability for femininity we can attribute that to a *culture* that confuses "love and violence" and "femininity and vulnerability." The problem is then one located in the matrix of culture, psyche, and body. As Rodriguez states, "I find that my husband didn't do what he did to me by himself. He had plenty of help. His parents, my parents, our society all worked together. They set us up from the start, to become the abuser and the abused."[60] Women's bodies and minds are both scarred *and* made by the gender hegemony of our culture. Many current writings in pastoral theology address the impact of negative cultural messages regarding the body, and return to the body as the site where the material effects of oppression and regulation are most apparent.[61] This increasing concern for the embodied life of persons in the context of culture, requires a shift from a theological anthropology informed primarily by theories of the psyche, to one which can also address and value the body as both an "artifact of culture"[62] and a site for resistance to that culture. This reconstructed theological anthropology must also offer a conceptualization of the interaction,

---

59. Such as Glaz and Moessner, *Women in Travail and Transition*; Miller-McLemore, "Subject and Practice;" Moessner, *Through the Eyes of Women*; Poling, *Abuse of Power*.

60. Rodriguez, *Time to Stop Pretending*, 9.

61. See several of the essays in Moessner, *Through the Eyes of Women*; Poling, *Abuse of Power*; Ramsay, "Compassionate Resistance."

62. A term used by Cooey, *Religious Imagination and the Body*.

or as I argue, the mutual constitution, of mind/body/culture, explicitly describing not only the interrelatedness of mind and body but also how they are made of and within particular cultural contexts.

In turn, this shifting paradigm is also changing the way pastoral theologians speak of care. Acknowledging the contribution culture makes to individual human suffering requires turning attention to cultural distributions and uses of power. With the inclusion of cultural analyses, the practice of care moves beyond individual therapeutic healing to advocacy for social change. For example, Christie Neuger suggests that pastoral counseling can be thought of as "political activism" and that the goal for feminist pastoral counseling is "transforming patriarchy."[63] James Poling's study on sexual violence as abuse of power sustained by social and psychological factors calls for analyses and transformations of individuals *and* communities.[64] Nancy Ramsay calls for "compassionate resistance" in the face of sexual abuse.[65] Others speak of resistance, empowerment, nurturing and liberation as functions of pastoral care and counseling.[66] If the root of suffering for a victim of intimate partner violence lies in a culture that objectifies and disempowers women, and not primarily in her individual psyche, then, we can be suppose that the best remedy to the suffering is social change. Psychological problems can then be interpreted as secondary to and/or emerging from societal and cultural injustices that have damaged the victim's psyche. Psychological and social resistance to oppression becomes a goal of pastoral care and thus a central concern for pastoral theology.[67]

However, these trends in pastoral theology raise further questions for a theological anthropology that wants to take seriously the context of culture in the formation and transformation of persons. Pastoral theologians must keep before them a concern for the material as well as the psychological lives of those who are suffering, and must think

63. Neuger, "Pastoral Counseling."

64. Poling, *Abuse of Power*.

65. Ramsay, "Compassionate Resistance."

66. Ali, *Survival and Liberation*; Miller-McLemore, "Subject and Practice," and "Feminist Theory in Pastoral Theology;" Ramsay, "Compassionate Resistance."

67. For some pastoral theological works in area of domestic violence, see Cooper-White, *Cry of Tamar*, and "An Emperor without Clothes"; Moessner, *Through the Eyes of Women*; Poling, *Abuse of Power*; Ramsay, "Compassionate Resistance."

about how these historically distinct categories are deeply interrelated with culture. As we examine human suffering through the lens of culture we find that the lines between individual/culture and mind/body continually shift and blur. We then have to ask how cultural discourses and practices themselves define these categorical constructions. And yet, if the person is deeply formed by culture and a victim of culture's oppressive regimes, then how and from where does the agency needed for resistance arise? Is there a "true" untainted person underneath the layers of culture? Do we look to the psyche for the agency needed to resist, change and heal and if so how do we avoid perpetuating the splits named above? Can we find agency in the body or in culture as well? How is the person formed and shaped in and through culture as both its victim and its agent? If we conceive of persons with too little agency we negate the *possibility* for change but too much agency negates the *necessity* for resistance. Is there a place outside of culture that exists within persons from which we can act, and if not, where does the power to resist come from? These questions about the "nature" of human personhood also raise theological questions about the relation of God and God's agency to culture and persons. Is there a "power of God," or an innate untainted "image of God," which remains distinct from culture and resides deeply within or completely transcends human beings? Is that the source of human agency?

Feminist Theory

These issues of culture/person, body/mind, resistance/agency that have arisen in work on intimate partner violence and pastoral theology have also made a deep impact on feminist theory. Early feminist theorizing opened up the category of "natural" womanhood. For instance, feminists made claims such as, girls were not born liking pink. Girls' preference for pink was exposed as a cultural construction, a norm born out of a gendered hegemony that was repeated so often that it had the effect of being "natural." Later attempts to define that which was core or essential to what it meant to be "woman" were inevitably challenged by women-of-color, lesbian women, and others who did not fit the Euro-American norm of "woman."[68] Much of what we thought was "just the way it is" has

---

68. See Moraga and Anzaldua, *This Bridge Called My Back*; Spelman, *Inessential Woman*.

been exposed to be "just the way we made it." Some feminist theorists now propose that the cultural construction goes all the way through, so to speak. That which is defined as "natural" or fixed is suspect, posing as a given but actually an effect of the continual reiteration of cultural norms and practices.

This project pursues this line of thinking through a feminist poststructuralist perspective and brings some of the debates in feminist theory to play in pastoral theology via the practice of care for victims of intimate partner violence. Poststructuralist interrogations develop around the themes of the constitutive nature of language and discursive effect, critique of universals, foundations, ontologies and binaries, suspicion of the "real" of the self, body, experience, and deconstruction of the unified, stable and autonomous subject. Debates in feminist theory swirl around fears that the "death of the subject" come just when women are beginning to gain subjectivity.[69] Theses critics of poststructuralism suggest that theorizing political and social change becomes impossible without a fundamental agency in subjects who can choose to resist or comply. Linda Alcoff accuses poststructuralism of colluding with the "dominant danger" of rendering human particularities irrelevant as it deconstructs the categories upon which political struggle has been based.[70] Nancy Fraser warns that feminists, in the face of structuralist accounts of language as a determinative symbol system, must keep a pragmatic approach to discourse which can illuminate possibilities for change.[71] These critics raise questions such as: How does a fully culturally constituted subject have the capacity to act against/outside/contrary to the constituting culture? If the subject is all discursive effect is there action that is not reiteration? If so, without a stable subject, without a resource outside of a culture intent upon reproducing itself, where does the agency needed to resist reside? If subjects are pure victims of culturally determined constructions there is, they fear, no capacity to resist.

The concrete concern for victims of oppression does raise "body" questions for poststructuralism. If bodies are not "real," if all is discourse, then what of the material? Feminists need to be able to ground theories for social change upon the concrete and visible signs of oppression

---

69. Hartsock, "Foucault on Power."
70. Alcoff, "Cultural Feminism."
71. Fraser, "Uses and Abuses."

such as bodies beaten, raped, and abused. The fear of losing the body to discourse is the fear of losing the focus on the material effects of oppression, of regulated bodies. Susan Bordo criticizes poststructuralism for its desire for a "view from nowhere" that seeks to transcend materiality with a worldview in which "language swallows everything up."[72] Feminist theorists have pointed out the problematic splits between mind/body and culture/nature in a culture that privileges mind over body and culture over nature and then identifies men with the mind/culture side of the split and women with the body/nature side. These critiques have provoked varying feminist responses including (a) pleas to value women's experience on the nature/body side of the split, (b) the inclusion of women on the historically more valued culture/mind side, and (c) an interrogation of the reality of the binaries themselves.[73] Bordo, while acknowledging the benefit of reading the body through a cultural interpretive lens, laments what she assesses as the body's move across the binary divide until it has disappeared, theorized away into culture/mind and with it political and social commitments to the real bodied lives of women.

A commitment to the body as central to feminist theorizing raises flags of caution in front of any theory that persuades toward an agency that "playfully" moves in "textual indeterminacy" through an array of possibilities, a cafeteria of identities, unlimited by biology or "nature." This projects a scene of "pure" agents, translating, interpreting, presenting, and representing culture at will and whim. As stated earlier, just as too little agency negates the possibility for change, too much agency negates the necessity for political and social change. The illusion of "being everywhere"[74] loses the reality of the partial, limited locatedness of lives lived in structures of power which limit the agency and subjectivity of some more than others.

Resistance is often talked about as if there is a place we can stand that is exempt from culture and from there gather the strength for resistance, the analytical tools for resistance, and the language of resistance. For instance, feminists sometimes claim that patriarchy has defined who women are but then seem to assume a place of "women's reality"

72. Bordo, *Unbearable Weight*.

73. For a good overview of this issue, see Jaggar and Bordo, *Gender/Body/Knowledge*.

74. Bordo, *Unbearable Weight*.

that somehow escapes being affected. In terms of inner self, this often gets described as "true" self, as if all the layers of culture can eventually be peeled away to find the "real" underneath. This is part of the assumption behind consciousness-raising. But is there a place to which we can run that escapes culture and from which resistance can be constructed, and if so where is it? Is there really a space deep within that remains untouched by patriarchal structures?

By definition, resistance is the act of withstanding or refusing to comply with a prevailing force. If patriarchy is seen as a prevailing force, the force that rules, then acts of resistance are acts that refuse to comply with or withstand the pressure of that force. Resistance assumes agency, which is the capacity or ability to act, to influence or have an effect. Usually it is assumed that agency is *self-determinative* action, that an "I" can determine or direct the action versus the action being the result of someone or something else acting upon the "I." For example, if someone pushes me and I fall, the fall is an action but it is not understood as an act of agency. It is an action that results from something being done *to* me, not something *I* do. If I stand up and push back, that is usually thought of as *my* action, a result of my agency. The crux of the problem that I raise lies in the *self-determinative* part of the definition of agency.

It can appear that theorizing political and social change becomes impossible without also theorizing a fundamental agency at the core of persons who can at some level *choose* to resist or comply. As I have pointed out above, social and political movements assume that the "victims" *do* have the power to resist or change the world. Feminism assumes that women who are oppressed and victimized by patriarchy can come together and act to undo that patriarchy. Underlying this assumption is another assumption that suggests that within persons is a core of agency for *self-determinative* action.

But if culture goes all the way through, if persons are constituted of culture and there is no space that escapes culture, then we must ask, where is the "self" that "determines" the action of resistance? A theory of cultural construction challenges the possibility that the source of agency is located in a fixed core, or "true," self. Cultural construction *seems* to point to two different conclusions regarding agency, both of which are problematic for feminists. First, it could be concluded that persons *are* absolutely determined by cultural forces and therefore have no agency at all. In this case it would be said that all action is determined by the power structures of culture. Therefore, in the case of patriarchy and women, women would be identified as so determined and victimized by culture that they are powerless to change it. Secondly, it could also be concluded that if all is constructed or made, and nothing is fixed or stable, then persons have complete freedom to re-construct, to make her or himself different at will. That which is defined as a social construction and not "natural," can be changed. This is like the arguments feminists have made about gender. Many of the characteristics that were thought to be "naturally" a part of what it means to be female (e.g. liking pink or being passive) have been exposed for being social constructions and since they are social constructions it is assumed that they can be changed. So, following this line of thinking, if human beings are fully socially constructed then we can "reinvent" ourselves.

As stated above either one of these conclusions is a problem for feminists. If we conceive of persons with too little agency we negate the *possibility* for change; we have no power to change anything; women are forever victims who must rely on others. But too much agency negates the *necessity* for resistance. Women do not need a political struggle if we can "choose" to be and act differently. One of the aims of this book is to find a way to speak of agency that keeps open the possibility and the necessity for change through resistance.

Toward a Pastoral Theological Anthropology

In the three perspectives presented above, intimate partner violence, pastoral theology, and feminist theory, I have identified questions that arise regarding human agency and the capacity to act in resistance. The questions twist and turn in their implications for one another and for the many that remain unasked. Even the phrasing and asking of certain questions and not others will shape any proposed response. Several poles around which the questions spiral can be identified: the depth and breadth of the cultural construction of persons, the origins and conditions of agency and constraint for human action, concerns for the body/mind of persons, and the agency and nature of human beings in relation to the same in God. These poles provide the foci for this book as I develop some propositional and contingent answers from which other questions will be raised.

This study holds that an adequate theological anthropology for a feminist pastoral theology, in order to address the process by which a person[75] is constructed in the context of culture, must keep central the body as well as the psyche and be able to identify the agency needed for resistance. The thesis of this project is that a theological concept of human personhood can identify persons as deeply constructed in and constituted of culture, both as psyche and body, whose agential capacities arise ambiguously from that same process of construction. In such a conception the person is formed of culture and yet, by virtue of that formation, also able to resist the culture which has brought the person into "being."[76]

I suggest that a theological anthropology constructed in the above manner is one way of making sense of personhood given the dynamics of intimate partner violence and is, likewise, one way of making sense of intimate partner violence via a theology of human personhood. Taking as a starting point, the experience of women in violent intimate relationships and the practice of those who work for their healing and liberation, this book pursues the above suggestions for thinking about the meaning of agential human persons in relation to culture, to self, to each other and to the divine.

Chapter Outline

Chapters 2 through 5 develop the theoretical argument for the pastoral theology of agency suggested above. The theological groundwork for this cultural construction of personhood will posit an ontological dy-

---

75. The terms "individual," "self," "person," and "subject" are often used interchangeably. In this context the terms "individual" and "self" suggest more autonomy and coherence than my theoretical approach allows. Butler, *Psychic Life of Power*. I agree with her that the use of the term "subject" emphasizes the cultural matrices which prescribe "subject" positions. Pastoral theologian Susan Dunlap, "Discourse Theory and Pastoral Theology," also takes this view. I use the term "person" here to keep before us a point that Bordo, *Unbearable Weight* makes, that there are no "subjects" that are not embodied persons.

76. I am suggesting, as does Judith Butler in "Contingent Foundations", that the constituted character and construction of the person is the precondition for agency. This position stands in contrast to the thought which assumes that agency must arise from an autonomous and stable subject. This point is a central concern in feminist theories of subjectivity. For some examples of these debates see Alcoff, "Cultural Feminism"; Bordo, *Unbearable Weight*, especially the introduction and "Postmodern Subjects"; Fraser, "Uses and Abuses"; Hartsock, "Foucault on Power."

namic interrelatedness based on the process theology of Loomer with the addition of a liberation theological perspective through the work of Soelle. Chapter 2 will establish this base using a critical correlational appropriation of Don Browning's method of deep metaphorical congruence, and argue that this posited ontology finds enough congruence with an expanded version of Faribairn's object relations theory and Butler's poststructuralist feminism that these three perspectives can be used together in a revised critical correlational mode to build a theological anthropology of agency.

Chapters 3 and 4 proceed, after a general discussion regarding the meaning of "construction," with an argument for the mutual constitution of mind, body and culture, drawn from the theories of Fairbairn, Butler and other relevant theorists. The thesis of the book suggests that any theology/theory of agency requires a theory of the cultural construction and constitution of personhood. These two chapters set out the details of this construction. Chapter 3 proposes a version of object relations theory that understands the psyche to be made of internal object relations which are constructed in and constituted of culture when culture is that which determines the content, form, and function of intersubjective relations and when intersubjectivity is the condition under which personhood develops. Chapter 4 then sets out the cultural construction and constitution of the material or body as both a creation of culture and creator of culture. In both the psyche and body dynamic interrelatedness is the power sustains and provokes these constructions.

The ambiguity of the power of dynamic interrelatedness and the core ambivalence in human personhood is highlighted in chapter 5 in the proposed theology of human agency. After a review of the questions and concerns for any feminist theory of agency the proposed theology proceeds around four points: the necessity of a theory of cultural construction and the possibility of reiterative failure, the ambiguity of power as that which can be used for both oppression and resistance, the constitutive outside as the site of agency for resistance, and the political bases upon and means by which agency is ascribed.

Chapter 6 concludes with some suggestions for a pastoral care that wants to foster agency and resistance for the healing, increased subjectivity and liberation of the suffering and thus the whole web of life. I offer four directions for this approach to pastoral care: attachment to the now and to more life; acknowledgement and acceptance of ambiguity; pursuit of the contradictions and exclusions made by culture and thus of individuals; and engagement in political analysis and advocacy.

2

Ontological Interrelatedness

IN THE PREVIOUS CHAPTER I SUGGESTED THAT PROCESS THEOLOGY, LIBeration theology, object relations theory, and feminist poststructuralist theories can be used together to support the thesis that a theological anthropology can identify persons as radically constructed of culture in a way that keeps both body and psyche central and identifies the agency needed for resistance. These theological and theoretical perspectives are the sources to which I turn for a pastoral theological construction from the context of care for persons in violent intimate relationships. This chapter will present some of the pertinent core assumptions of the various perspectives, addressing points of congruence and departure between them.

The method by which I approach sources from different fields follows Carrie Doehring's "critical correlational" method for feminist pastoral theology.[1] A critical correlational method asserts that neither the sources and norms from theological studies nor those from feminist studies and psychological studies should take precedence over the other. Such an approach does not negate the ultimate purpose of theological contribution behind this project but allows those theological contributions to include insights and questions from other fields at a level of significance equal to those from theology. Feminist pastoral theology in this vein suggests exploring these various fields in a back and forth movement, noting points of agreement and areas of contribution to one another, and retaining the tensions that exist between them. It appreciates the differences in purposes and interests in each field while it also seeks to bring those fields into conversation with each other. A critical correlational approach also meets Seward Hiltner's

---

1. Doehring, "Feminist Pastoral Theology."

criteria for a methodological use of theology and psychological and social scientific theories. Hiltner insists on a "two way street" between theology and other theories by which both questions and answers are raised across the fields to each other.[2] Like Doehring, I am using a poststructuralist norm for considering truth claims which suggests that all claims to truth are partial and contingent upon historical, political, and cultural context. While provisional truth claims will be proposed, those provisional truths are not necessarily nor exclusively found at points of agreement between fields of study but may just as likely appear in the points of disagreement.

This chapter will, by way of critical correlation, explore the core assumptions and "deep metaphors"[3] in process theology, liberation theology, object relations theory, and poststructuralist feminist theory in their particular treatment of a posited ontological[4] interrelatedness and its implications for what it means to be human. Don Browning suggests that underlying metaphors or visions of ultimacy can be unearthed in psychologies, and, I suggest, in theories from other disciplines as well. These metaphorical visions answer the questions of what is most ultimate and what kind of world we live in. In other words they are ontological assumptions about the nature of reality itself and therefore theological to the extent that theologies are theories of ontological realities. At a basic level,[5] psychologies hold a kind of religious and theological thinking evident in their underlying ontological assumptions, or "deep metaphors." We can then judge the congruency and incongruency between two particular stances, one in theory and the other theology.

I am looking at the ontologies of particular theologies and theories from the assumption that there must be enough congruity at this basic level to hold them in conversation with each other. Browning goes on to suggest that these metaphors of ultimacy point toward obligations for practice, that they directly influence "what we think we are obli-

---

2. Hiltner, *Preface to Pastoral Theology*, 223n19.

3. Browning, *Religous Thought*, 9.

4. From a poststructuralist perspective it is important to be clear that these are "posited" ontologies, temporary and contingent interpretations for the purpose of discussion, not explanations of what "really is."

5. Browning, *Religious Thought*, calls the level of metaphor/vision the first level of practical moral thinking as we try to decide what it is that we should do.

gated to do."[6] The purpose of this chapter is to review in three different fields, and specific lenses within those fields, the deep metaphors of an ultimate web of interrelatedness for what they imply separately and together about the nature of being human and how it is that we have or obtain the agency needed to "act." Process theologian Bernard Loomer and liberation theologian Dorothee Soelle provide the primary theological perspectives. Object relations theory is looked at through the theory of W. R. D. Fairbairn and various feminist constructive critiques. The primary feminist poststructuralist offered is through the work of Judith Butler. These theologians and theorists have been chosen for their clear interest in deep interrelatedness as core to their particular understandings, which is not to imply that they each see interrelatedness in the same manner. Their varied foundations in posited ontologies of interrelatedness makes each of these theorists particularly useful in positing a theological understanding of human persons as constructed in/by and constituted of culture. As we will see, an argument for radical cultural construction implies and requires the support of theologies/theories grounded in a deep dynamic interrelatedness that can form a framework for an interpretation of human personhood not as substance or essence but as intersubjective process through which the mutual constitution of mind/body/culture/person occurs.[7] Thus this chapter looks at the deep vision of interrelatedness in the theologies/theories described above.

Theological Interrelatedness

I begin with a discussion of interrelatedness as understood in process theologian Bernard Loomer's extrapolation of Whitehead's process thought into a "process relational mode of thinking"[8] about God as the "organic restlessness"[9] of the web of creation. In his explication of the web of interrelatedness Loomer falls short of exploring the sociopolitical ramifications of certain structures of relationship in that web, an endeavor that is necessary in order to speak to the relational injustices that sustain and create intimate partner violence. Soelle's liberation the-

6. Ibid., 20.
7. The specifics will be detailed in next chapter.
8. Loomer, "Size of God," 23.
9. Ibid., 41.

ology is congruent enough with Loomer that her theology of liberation can work in conjunction with process theology, bringing to it a strong cultural analysis. Thus this section explores these theological perspectives on interrelatedness and some of their implications for a theological anthropology.

A Process View

Loomer emphasizes two ontological categories, extracted from Whitehead, upon which his theology is built, that of "becoming" and "relatedness."[10] In process theology, not surprisingly so, process is ultimate. "Becoming" is that which beyond nothing exists. There is no "being" before "becoming," no being that puts becoming into motion. The one given about reality, about the way things are, is, in fact, that they are always becoming something new. According to Loomer there is no final cause beyond becoming. "[T]he reasons why things are the way they are and behave as they do are to be found within the things themselves and their relationships (including the factor of chance) to each other."[11] The reason for things is "found in the things themselves," in the actual entities, that are event not substance, which makes things as they are. Whitehead states it this way: "The final facts are, all alike, actual entities; and these actual entities are drops of experience, complex and interdependent."[12] The process of becoming moves through the actuality of occasions of experience, "droplets" of experience,[13] that are in themselves unique and unchangeable, emerging from the actual occasions of the past and immediately superceded by the future, a minute point of transition between the past and the future. Each actual occasion is what it is but is then left behind as it gives way to the successive string of more actual occasions. Each event is immediately surpassed by another event. Actuality, that which is fact about life itself, is the dynamic process that brings things into "being," being that appears as fixed substance but is in actuality a coming together, a "concresecence,"[14]

---

10. Ibid., 28.
11. Ibid., 25.
12. Whitehead, *Process and Reality*, 18.
13. A phrase adapted from William James's "drops of experience" and often used in process theology to describe actual occasions.
14. Whitehead, *Process and Reality*, 21.

of occasions of experience that is never in the most minute moment of time the same as in the moment preceding or following it. The actual occasion does not endure into the future or change the past but its effect lasts into perpetuity. There is no actual occasion that is not derived from other actual occasions and therefore affected by those preceding actualities.[15]

Experience as used here, is beyond our cognition or awareness, for these actual occasions are occurring everywhere, all the time. They are what life and the living are made of, rooted in the processes of physical feeling which is experience.[16] Experience is not merely sense perception, that which we know through hearing, tasting, seeing, feeling, but what Whitehead calls a "vague totality" of experiential data.[17] It is also not limited to conceptual perception which is a response to the experience of actual occasions. Both sense and conceptual perception require an abstraction from the "vague totality," a process of selection, in which some experience is background and other is highlighted. The totality of experience is there and Loomer suggests we can develop a "conceptual sensitivity"[18] to the whole of experience but physical experience requires of us an interplay of sense and conceptual experience in order to bring to life structure, form and function. What we might normally call a feeling, idea, person, or behavior arises from a coalescence of actual occasions into a togetherness that then moves in some common way. In process thought this togetherness of actual occasions is called a "nexus" and the "nexus" in a common mode is a "society."[19] That called mind, matter, tree or person is a society, or a society of societies within societies, a coming together of these drops of experience in a pattern that gives a person, for instance, structure and form.

The question must be asked whether or not there is an aim or purpose undergirding and directing this process of becoming. For in each actual occasion there is pure potential for something more but is there a form or order that determines or directs the "creative impulse"

---

15. Ibid.

16. Loomer, "Size of God," 24.

17. Whitehead, *Modes of Thought*, 109. Whitehead is distinguishing his use of "experience" from Hume's.

18. Loomer, "Size of God," 24.

19. For more explanation of nexus and society, see Loomer, "Size of God," 28, and Whitehead, *Process and Reality*, chapters 2 and 3.

in which the many become one and are increased by one?[20] According to Loomer the answer is no. There is only the aim to "more." But, more what? Loomer's thought might respond, more of what *is*, which are actual occasions that are what life is made of. The aim to more, is an aim to more life. The pure potential for anything in every drop of experience is not determined in a particular direction except in the direction of "more." "At the heart of things there is a passion or a restlessness to move toward the increase in value, to achieve the 'more,' to transform what is into a 'better.'"[21] The aims or purpose of these actual occasions engaged in the process of becoming are multiple, not infinite but more than is possible to count or comprehend.

> Some [aims and purposes] are compatible, some are cooperative, and others are mutually enhancing. Others are contraries, and still others are mutually contradictory and destructive. In and through, because of, and in spite of this diversity and these contradictions and this disorder, there persists a restlessness or a tropism not only to live, but to live well and to live better (Whitehead). This passion carries its own appeal, its own authority and warrant, and its own limited strength to fulfill itself in due season.[22]

For Loomer this passion for more carries within it a norm for greater stature, by which we can judge the adequacy of certain directions the movement toward "more" might take. The movement can be toward more good or more evil (a point we will return to later in this section). Stature provides the criteria by which the good can be judged. More stature (or size) means more depth and breadth, more potential and possibility. In terms of the individual, Loomer defines stature as "the volume of life you can take into your being and still maintain your integrity and individuality, the intensity and variety of outlook you can entertain in the unity of your being without feeling defensive or insecure."[23]

This passion for more life is inherent to the "web of interrelatedness." It is the web of interrelatedness that is, according to Loomer,

---

20. Whitehead, *Process and Reality*.
21. Loomer, "Size of God," 31.
22. Whitehead, *Function of Reason*, 8; quoted in Loomer, "Size of God," 42.
23. Loomer, "S-I-Z-E," 6.

the primary principle of the "ultimacy of becoming."[24] The principle by which becoming can be understood is the principle of the interrelatedness of every event, and thus of all creation. It is in "the things themselves and their *relationships* (including the factor of chance) to each other" (italics mine) that we find the reason for the character and behavior of things.[25] Loomer emphasizes not only the dynamic process that is the basis for all that is, but also the principle of organic interrelatedness through which process moves. In the web of life each thing is related to every other. There is no movement of one that does not affect all others, no drop of experience that does not change the whole of the web of life, at least in some minute way. As Whitehead states it, "every entity pervades the whole world."[26]

Interrelatedness is "equiprimordial" to "becoming." Together they are taken to be the fundamental nature of reality.

> If we speak of the ultimacy of becoming, then we must speak of the primacy of relatedness. Becoming may be the more inclusive category, but without the presence of dynamic relationships from which actualities emerge, the notion of becoming would be empty of content. Neither becoming nor relatedness is an emergent. They are equiprimordial.
>
> Furthermore, even though becoming is the most inclusive category, relatedness has a priority in value. Process exists for the sake of relationships.[27]

As ontological principles relatedness and becoming give form to reality and all discussion of the "nature" of things, including persons, will begin with these two fundamental facts.[28]

Interconnection is then the constitutive principle of which and by which life and any "being" in the web of life is formed. The constitution of one actual entity arises from other actual entities. Loomer describes this principle:

---

24. Loomer, "Size of God."
25. Ibid., 25.
26. Whitehead, *Process and Reality*, 28.
27. Loomer, "Size of God," 31.
28. Facts as used here should be understood as changing propositions. Relatedness and becoming as fundamental facts imply a dynamism as fact, not fact as fixed and unchanging, or as ultimate truth.

> We feed upon each other in all the dimensions of our lives
> ... physically, emotionally, intellectually, spiritually. We create
> each other. We live within relationships. We live within interlaced fields of energy or relational webs of interconnectedness.
> Individuals are created within these fields and their possibilities
> emerge within these interrelationships.[29]

It follows that in order to "know" or understand a thing we must understand the whole web of relations and the historic chain of actual occasions[30] from which that "thing" emerged. To do less than that limits our understanding and circumscribes the thing itself to less than it is, what Whitehead calls an "abstraction." There is not a substantive entity that then becomes related to another substantive entity but rather, in the mode of thinking presented here, only actual occasions which come into existence in, out of and with relatedness with each other. Enduring objects or structures appear fixed but in actuality are in constant flux. That which appears self-defined and self-sufficient is only itself in relation to others. The unity or order that contributes to the appearance of fixity emerges from the interdependent relations that constitute an event.

At the heart of the web is a restlessness, an energy, a passion for more, the power of life. The power of life arises from the interconnectedness of life. The power of the web has no inherent "goodness" or "badness," it simply is. "To be alive is to exercise power in some degree."[31] Power may be exercised either for good or for evil, the greater potential for one is the greater potential for the other, as Loomer's oft references to Reinhold Niebuhr point out. Power used for evil cannot destroy the web, because the web is life and power emerges from the web, in other words if there is no web there is no power at all, for good or evil, but power can be directed to "enhance or impoverish" the web of relations.[32] Therefore, by his own terms, Loomer's "drive for more" is also a drive for less. The restlessness at the heart of creation requires movement

---

29. Loomer, "Size of God," 32.

30. Neither Whitehead nor Loomer directly considers the "history" of actual occasions but William Dean, "Deconstruction and Process Theology," suggests that we must have an historical method. As we will see, liberation theology points us in that direction, as does poststructuralist thought.

31. Loomer, "Two Conceptions of Power," 5.

32. Loomer, "On Committing Yourself to a Relationship."

toward more or less, toward more stature and enriched relationship, or toward less, diminished relationship. As I will later elaborate, both the movements toward more and toward less are rooted in our need for continuing relatedness, and since continuing relatedness is equivalent to continuous life, we can also say these movements are rooted in our need for survival.

Loomer lays out two possibilities for the use of power, "unilateral" and "relational," the first results in diminished size and the latter in greater stature.[33] Power used unilaterally seeks control over another, to shape and mold one to the agenda of another. According to Loomer this use of power diminishes the relational web. The "size" or stature of one might appear to be enhanced but its appearance of greater size is at the diminishment of the other and thus could be called a false stature, or perhaps a fragile one, since it rests on a tenuous relation in which one apparently grows while the other decays. From the point of view of life and relation as coextensive then the total decay or destruction of one ultimately results in the decay and destruction of the other. Unilateral use of power is not only other destructive but self-destructive. On the other hand, relational power, or what I prefer to call mutual power,[34] works through the taking in of the other, of claiming as fully as possible the reality of "mutual internal relations"[35] in which we all exist.

> This is a relationship of mutually influencing and being influenced, of mutually giving and receiving, of mutually making claims and permitting and enabling others to make their claims. This is a relation of mutuality which embraces all the dimensions and kinds of inequality that the human spirit is heir to. The principle of equality most profoundly means that we are equally dependent on the constitutive relationships that create us, however relatively unequal we are in our various strengths, including our ability to exemplify the fullness and concreteness of this kind of power.[36]

---

33. Loomer, "Two Conceptions of Power."

34. Loomer uses the term "relational power" but I find this term problematic since by his own terms all power is relational whether it is used relationally or unilaterally.

35. Loomer, "Two Conceptions of Power," 22.

36. Ibid.

By this use of power the stature of one increases as the one can take in the "more" or the influence of the other. This use of power in mutuality works for the "enlargement" of all.[37]

Thinking in terms of the enlargement of all pushes us to think beyond the relationships of two persons toward thinking about how relationships between persons are related to the relationship between all persons. And thinking about relationships between all persons necessarily requires attention to the social and cultural structures that shape those relationships. Loomer does not articulate a soiciocultural reading of his relational mode of thinking but a turn to liberation theology, via Dorothee Soelle, can assist in such a reading.

Including a Liberation Perspective

Liberation theology as exemplified here in the work of Dorothee Soelle, picks up the process theme of an ontology of dynamic interrelatedness but the focus of the liberation perspective is not on metaphysics but the concrete character of the web and the direction of the dynamism.[38] Soelle refers to creation as a "work in progress."[39] In other words, the creativity involved in creation continues. Creation of the earth, persons, or any living "being," is not an event that happened and now remains in a finished state, but is on-going and ever becoming. One is not created and then left bereft of creative energy but instead emerges from, in and through creativity and continues in the creating. Soelle's movement of creativity which can be seen as a version of process' "becoming," is the basis of life and all that is.

Creativity moves through a web of creation in which all living things are connected, thus movement in one affects the other, what Soelle calls a "dynamic holism."[40] The influence of process thought's *event* focus and process and feminist theology's *relationhip* focus is evident in Soelle's ontology of "being-in-relationship," existence as interaction, rather than "being-in-itself," which frames existence as an independent

---

37. Ibid., 27.

38. For specific references to process thought, see Soelle and Cloyes, *To Work and to Love*, 25.

39. Soelle, *Thinking About God*, 51.

40. Soelle, *Theology for Skeptics*, 119.

substance.⁴¹ Soelle's ontological assumption of the interconnection of life is most clearly seen in her discussions of the effects of oppression and the destruction of the earth and its creatures. She points out the interrelatedness of the social and personal in *To Work and to Love*:

> When labor is geared to exchange value and the universal need for money, our human relationships are not immune to the laws of exchange production. It is an illusion to think that people who work from nine to five for exchange value, treating their own work and their relationships to co-workers and products according to the rules of commodity exchange, can then return home and relate to others and to themselves as unalienated human beings capable of fulfilling their suppressed needs.⁴²

When the social context is unjust, the person is harmed. When one area of life is limited, all areas are limited. In her work on suffering Soelle's sense of deep interrelatedness is apparent as she continually points out the pain we all carry when another is suffering. "There is no alien sorrow, we are a part of it, we share in it."⁴³

Like process theology, liberation theology is focused on the events of experience, but in liberation theology *experience* would refer to the broader process category of societies within societies and their relation to each other. Liberation theology leans heavily on "experience" as a test for the "true" nature of things and of God. Liberation theology might ask how does a person's *experience* of a particular theological idea speak to the truth of that idea?⁴⁴ The web of interconnection must be examined for historical and present context. Although in agreement with the process perspective that all is interrelated, that the present is implicated in the past and that the future is implicated in the present, this does not go far enough. We must explore the character of the web, how it is structured, how persons and peoples concretely experience life in it, and the nature of the historic chain of interaction from which the present has emerged. Soelle's liberation theology draws on, in addition to process thought, philosophical materialism to emphasize the experience of bodily matter, not only ideals or mind, but concrete embodied

---

41. Soelle, *Thinking About God*, 180.
42. Soelle and Cloyes, *To Work and to Love*, 116.
43. Soelle, *Suffering*, 172.
44. For Soelle's use of experience, see Soelle, *Thinking About God*, 99ff., and *Strength of the Weak*, 91–105.

interaction. She states that "reality is matter in motion, and we do not need other principles in order to explain it."[45] The material is the real and matter-in-motion is the ultimate reality.

As Marjorie Suchocki points out, Loomer's norm of stature is comparable to liberation theology's norm of liberation.[46] Soelle's primary concern is precisely at this point in the process of becoming—which direction shall the becoming, or the change, take? The passion for more at the heart of becoming might be described by Soelle as a passion for freedom, for liberation from bondage. She suggests that ontology must be interpreted in light of liberation.[47]

> Creation faith is susceptible to the danger of 'cheap reconciliation' whereby we are asked to live as if we did not require freeing from present, unjust orders, as if the presumption of a universal transhistorical order were sufficient in itself for human life, and as if the God of nature had triumphed over the God of history. The oppressed have an epistemological advantage: They wait for a greater God. Creation is not yet finished. Both projects, the historical and the ontological, are aimed at the freedom of the human being, and it is one of the claims of this book [*To Work and To Love*] that both projects need human agency. Participation in the ontological project of creation—human liberation—is possible only for the Exodus people, who have experienced at least once the liberating empowerment of the source of life. The universal source of life is not endlessly available to us, but, as the Jewish and Christian traditions claim, comes to us through particular historical events.[48]

In other words the nature of reality, of existence itself, must be understood through the movement of history, the continuation of the creative increase of freedom, or, as she states elsewhere,[49] the increase of subjectivity for all persons. There is more to happen, more to be done, more that is required for human life and this movement toward more is also movement toward liberation, is the "ontological project" or the nature of reality itself, and is evident in "particular historical events." In Loomer's terms the evidence of liberation might be the increase of stature, and

45. Soelle and Cloyes, *To Work and to Love*, 27.
46. Suchocki, "Radical Empiricism."
47. Soelle and Cloyes, *To Work and to Love*, 7–21.
48. Ibid., 10.
49. Soelle, *Creative Disobedience*.

to work toward greater stature can be considered work toward greater liberation. Soelle also implies in this passage that God and history, as particular and in progress, are deeply interrelated, as are then, God and humanity. An ontology that "needs human agency" implies a God that needs human agency which acts in the concrete and particular context of human life, a point to which we will return shortly.

Soelle's particular ontological concern is whether or not the web is working for oppression or liberation, for more life for *all* creation or for a particular person or group. It is not that one group can indeed have life at the expense of another but that one group can attempt to amass power and social/cultural privilege in order to build something that is purported by the more powerful to be life. Just as Loomer's unilateral power which makes one appear larger while the other is diminished ultimately results in diminishment for all, Soelle suggests that the appearance of increased subjectivity for one who gains that appearance through the objectification and oppression of another lives in a false sense of fulfillment plagued by fear and guilt.[50] Soelle, like Loomer, speaks of two kinds of power, that of authority and that of mutual relationship.[51] The power of authority, "evil power,"[52] operates through an unjust ordering of the web that ultimately diminishes life in connection. For instance, the effect on human beings of sexism, racism, or imperialism, "deprives them of their share in the power of life by making them completely powerless and subjecting them to the total domination of others."[53] The "good power" of sharing, mutuality, and reciprocality bring more relatedness, more life, and more of the creative liberating power of God into being.

Here, in the identification of God related to good power and evil power, we arrive at a crucial difference between Loomer's and Soelle's theological positions. While in both cases God and the world are closely identified with each other, Soelle identifies God with the goodness or liberative power of the created world and Loomer identifies God with the whole of the world, including both the power toward good and the power toward evil. Soelle certainly agrees that evil power is present and

50. Ibid., 43–46.
51. Soelle and Cloyes, *To Work and to Love*, 27.
52. Ibid.
53. Soelle, *Thinking About God*. Soelle makes this statement in reference to Apartheid but her implication is that it applies to all forms of oppression.

active in the world, but sees that power as antithetical to the God of liberation, which moves solely in resistance to evil.

Two Ways of Thinking About God

In process theology, God is deeply related to creation, responsive to the dynamics of the historical situation, and event rather than substance. Soelle finds in these aspects of process thought a means to solve the problem of a god who reinforces the dualistic split between subject and object which sustains a paradigm of power by authoritative control. We recall that Soelle believes that this kind of power, which is evil and ultimately diminishes life, is sustained in unjust social orders such as sexism, racism, and classism where one group is objectified and oppressed by another. A "wholly other," separate, transcendent, unresponsive, and unchanging God deifies the subject/object split; while a God deeply immanent, related in history and creation, heals the split and suggests a norm of relatedness rather than separateness.[54] An ontology of being-in-itself, and not being-in-relationship, reflects a subject/object split that inevitably leads to domination by the subject and subordination of the object. The "subjugation of the object by a relationless subject . . . leads to a culture of injustice."[55] The rhetoric of obedience to a relationless God arises from postulating God as an independent subject without needs, who demands the subjugation of its objects. Soelle suggests a move in our theological paradigms from obedience, constraint, and sacrifice to spontaneity, subjectivity, and freedom. An increase in one's subjectivity will not threaten the subjectivity of another but will enlarge the whole because of interdependence.[56] This kind of thinking about God can also resolve the problem of a split between spirit and matter, or mind and body, because it poses God as not only deeply concerned with the material, but known and active through immersion in the concrete matter of life.[57]

Soelle, however, does not identify God with the whole of creation but rather with that aspect of creation that is fundamentally good and

---

54. Soelle and Cloyes, *To Work and to Love*, 13ff. See 25–26 for specific references to process thought.
55. Soelle, *Thinking About God*, 125.
56. Soelle, *Creative Disobedience*, 34.
57. Soelle, *Thinking About God*, 151ff.

which is the essence of life. In spite of her focus on suffering and the need to redeem injustice, she carries a fundamental optimism about the ultimate goodness of God and creation, including human persons. Loomer on the other hand, and parting not only with liberation theologians but with many process theologians, identifies God fully with the world. In other words, the fullness of the world, including its good and its bad, equals the fullness of God and the fullness of God equals the fullness of the world. Soelle wants to limit God to that which is good and liberative while Loomer proposes a "larger" God, one that includes the good and the bad, the liberative and the oppressive. This difference will be crucial for understanding the direction of my thesis for a theological anthropology that includes an ambiguous agency.

For Soelle, there are two forms of power, one of which is God's power and the other which is not. God's power is the relatedness at the origins of life itself and evil power is power that acts against relatedness for separation and domination. She states,

> I slowly came to understand that outside the power to shout and shoot, outside the power of the imperium, there are yet other forms of power which arise out of our being bound up with the ground of life. The grass that grows into the light through the asphalt also has power: not power to command, to rule, to manipulate, but a power which comes to life from a relationship. How can we distinguish good power, the power of life, from evil power, the power to dominate? This question is central for a feminist and thus humane way of thinking. The most important criterion for answering it is that good power is shared power, power which distributes itself, which involves others, which grows through dispersion and does not become less. . . . Real relationship means that an exchange takes place and that people gain a share in the creative, good, non-compelling power of God.[58]

The difficulty with this position is that if one is to posit life as necessarily and ontologically interrelated and whole, and one wants to avoid ontological dualisms, and if God is the origin of life, the ontological itself, then God must be interrelationship, wholeness, all that is of life or reality itself. To pose good power and bad power is to suggest that either there is an ontological dualism at the origins of life or that there is one

---

58. Ibid., 188.

power that then can take multiple forms, which we may label good and/ or bad. To take the latter position and to retain a notion of God as that which is ontologically ultimate, would suggest that God is the power of life, which is interrelationality, that then may act for good or evil. In a sense this is suggesting that the power of God is neutral in value or valueless in of itself except to the extent that it is primary and ultimate, and essentially ambiguous. It is how we act with and from that power that then becomes the context within which a value of good or evil is assigned. Assigning value is, after all, a human practice. Soelle writes,

> If we are serious about understanding God's being in social terms, thinking of God as the power at the beginning, the power of relationship, then the continuation of creation depends on the strength of love among human beings. Whether or not the nuclear winter comes depends on how many people rise from the death of unrelatedness and are converted. God lures anew each day, to repent.[59]

If the power at the beginning is relationship, then Soelle is right that unrelatedness is death. If life is always by definition interrelationship then there is no life that is unrelated, in truth then, we should speak of more or less relatedness, or perhaps stronger or weaker, or the power of relatedness used for more life or less life, not relatedness and unrelatedness. Thus we arrive at the suggestion that life itself, and thus interrelatedness, is more ambiguous at its core than connotated by a God power that is fundamentally good.

Loomer makes an argument for an ambiguous God in an attempt to address problems similar to those raised above, but his framework raises a problem internal to process thought. Not unlike Soelle, for Loomer an "abstract," independent and autonomous God is inadequate and at odds with experience and the process view of reality. As an "abstraction"[60] God is not concrete actuality but partial and limited experience abstracted from context and relations, pulled into the foreground of the totality of experience for emphasis and partial understanding. But the whole is only understood in context of the relation to others. As one aspect of the world—goodness—God is an abstraction and therefore inadequate, according to Loomer, to be called God.

---

59. Ibid., 195.
60. Whitehead, *Modes of Thought*.

> If God is to be spoken of as something more than an ideal or a principle (that is as something more than a final or formal cause), then it follows that the being of God must be identified in some sense with the being of the world and its creatures. ... If God has a reality beyond that of an abstraction, then God is in some sense concretely actual. As an actuality or a group of actualities God is then to be identified either with a part or with the totality of the concrete, actual world, including its possibilities.[61]

Loomer argues that a god identified as the totality is larger in stature than a god who is but one aspect of that totality and if stature, as per our earlier discussion, is the norm by which we might choose one direction over another then a god of greater stature is preferable to a god of smaller stature.

To speak of God as the totality of the web of interconnected life is to make God truly "all" powerful, not in the way of authoritative imperialism, but in the sense that "all" power arises from the "ultimacy of becoming and the primacy of relationship." Granted this power holds within it the possibility of good and of evil, enrichment or diminishment of life, but this we must accept if we are to have a concrete actual God who is of the world, not above or independent from the world. This God is deeply and radically involved in the material reality of life.

> In terms of this analysis, God as wholeness is to be identified with the concrete, interconnected totality of this struggling, imperfect, unfinished, and evolving societal web. ... God is not only, or perhaps even primarily, the divine eros, understood as a conceptual appetition toward the good. This again is an abstract mode of operation that has its important role: but more concretely, God is expressed as the organic restlessness of the whole body of creation, as this drive is unequally exemplified in the several parts of this societal web. This discontent, which is an expression of the essential "spirit" of any creature, may exemplify itself as an expansive urge toward greater good. It may also become a passion for greater evil that, however, disguised or rationalized as a greater good, also has its attractiveness. Furthermore, God is not only the ultimate end for which all things exist. God is also the shape and stuff of existence.[62]

---

61. Loomer, "Size of God," 23.
62. Ibid., 41.

Although this is a basic and crucial difference between the theological view points of Soelle and Loomer, in both instances we are left with the clear mandate to take human action seriously, for in both cases God's being and human being, God's activity and human activity, are inextricably linked.

Implications for a Theological Anthropology

I have stated that a theological ontology of interrelatedness as posed by these two perspectives shall be the primary theological sources from which we will construct a theological anthropology. The preceding discussion suggests an anthropology that holds event as constitutive and historical, interrelatedness as requisite to life itself, the divine/human relationship, including divine/human agency, as mutually dependent and coexistent. In addition, given the discussion above, I am positing a theological anthropology that sees the power of life in the web of interconnectedness as fundamentally ambiguous. At this point a brief discussion will lay the theological groundwork for development of these ideas in forthcoming chapters.

First, person as hereby suggested, is event rather than substance, dynamic rather than fixed. The society of actual occasions, or rather societies within societies, that make up a person is at no moment the same as the moment before. As Loomer states,

> In everyday usage, when we refer to an individual we normally have in mind an enduring person and not a self as a momentary occasion. As units of energy these instances of becoming are the very 'stuff' of existence. They constitute the 'substantial' side of things. The individual process of becoming is the concrete actual reality. The actuality consists of the becoming. All else, forms, structures, and qualities, are components of processes.[63]

The person has the effect of unity, permanence, and coherence but the actuality is that persons are always under construction. The person emerges from an "historical route of occasions"[64] which determines the present unity. This person/event merging and determined by the totality of past experience is not simple; the historic route is an enormously complex web of experience across time and space that synthesizes for

---

63. Loomer, "Conception of Creation," 322.
64. Loomer, "Size of God," 29.

the minutest of moments before being superseded by the next actual occasion. Persons are determined and limited by the past but we should not infer that persons are predictable or absolutely determined. The potential for the future of each actual occasion is not infinite but certainly more than we can count. There are also structures and patterns by which events, and thus persons, are organized within themselves and between themselves and others. These patterns and structures emerge from and endure through the processes themselves.[65]

This perspective on human persons places high value on experience, including physical experience. As Soelle says, we are "made from dust."[66] The experience of mind and body are coemergent and require mutual consideration. There is no place in this schema to prize the soul or mind as above, or more godly, than the body or even as separate from the body. An emphasis on mind over matter makes little sense, since mind and matter are coexistent, co-emergent, more side-by-side than one over the other. They always shape and form each other. There is no person who *has* a body but rather a person is her/his body from which the mind or spirit is only linguistically, not actually, separable. The "dust" factor requires us to consider human persons in the fullness of our material life, including our dependence on one another.

The person is an emergent within concrete historical context, and in a pattern and structure of interrelatedness to other events that we can examine and about which we can make determinations. We come into being in relationship to others. There is no person that is not related for interrelatedness and interdependence are the essence of life itself. It is not that persons have relationships but that a person is her/his relationships. As Loomer states it, ". . . the self is constituted in large part by its relations, that the self not only lives in community but the community quite literally lives within the self, and that both the self and the community are emergents from the causual [sic] efficaciousness of relations."[67] In order to understand the "nature" of human personhood we must understand the web of relations in and through which the person has being. Not unlike the feminist maxim, "the personal is political," the individual is cultural, to the extent that culture is an expression of

---

65. Ibid., 28–29.
66. Soelle and Cloyes, *To Work and to Love*.
67. Loomer, "Theology in the American Grain," 146.

the structure, patterns, and symbols of human life in relation to other human beings, to the earth, and to the cosmos. To examine and evaluate the social is to examine and evaluate the person. To change the person is to change the social, and to change the social is to change the person.

Inherent in this proposition also lies the implication that more relatedness means more person, more life, and, if we accept God as the totality of the web, more God. The power that gives persons life is the power of the on-going work of interrelatedness that suggests that the strengthening and enrichment of relations, by definition, strengthens and enriches the lives of persons. The criteria by which relations can be judged to do just that are, as described in our discussion of liberation and the use of power, determined by the self-evidence of the web itself and can be described as more stature, increased subjectivity, or liberation which emerges from relatedness structured in mutuality. The "goodness" of life is rooted in and enabled by interrelatedness in a "world of becoming,"[68] not the other way around. Our freedom emerges from interrelateness, or as Loomer says, "We are related to be free,"[69] not free to be related. We love because we are interrelated, not that interrelated because we love.

If God is this interrelated world of becomingness and human persons are constituted of this same world then the separation between the divine and human is at least undetectable and at most nonexistent. This is not to say that God is equal to humanity, but to identify God with the totality of the world is to include humanity in God in humanity's totality.[70] God's being, as "being-in-relationship" is also the "being" of human persons. Soelle speaks of the "sameness" of God and humanity rather than "otherness." "Under the 'sameness' rubric, the emphasis is on the God with us, the God within us, and the God with whom we can identify and finally be united."[71] The activity of God is to be found in the activity of the world, and the activity of persons is understood as the activity of God.

---

68. Ibid., 147.

69. Loomer, "Size of God," 51, and "Theology in the American Grain," 34–35.

70. I am speaking of humanity because the focus of this work is on human personhood but I do not mean to imply that the totality does not include the non-human world. For more in that vein, see McFague, *Body of God*.

71. Soelle and Cloyes, *To Work and to Love*, 44.

This creative activity born out of interrelatedness is, however, not always "good" since to increase the stature or subjectivity of God and persons is to also increase the possibility of "bad" or less stature and subjectivity. Power, which means the power of relatedness which means God, is fundamentally ambiguous, and can be directed for good or evil. Thus, contrary to Soelle's fundamental optimism, persons are, at their core, ambiguous as well. This should not be construed as a pessimistic view of humanity, which would assume more evil than good, but instead a kind of ambivalence, the power to do good or bad. If "doing" and "being" are indivisbly linked in what it means to be a person then I am suggesting that persons are essentially ambiguous. We will further develop this concept of ambiguity in the following chapters but for now the point is that God, the "whole" of the world, and therefore human persons, are of a power that must be ambiguous or else it would not be whole and would not be the power of interrelations. Although Soelle would disagree with expanding this ambiguity to God, her following statement suggests one direction for thinking of this ambiguity in a positive fashion.

> Every expression of life, for example every human relationship, every creative activity, should be 'whole'—that is to say all our powers should be involved in it. The more of myself I have to deny, repress and stifle in a relationship, the more partial and impoverished the relationship will be. One-dimensionality is the expression of this prevailing impoverishment, and destruction.[72]

As we will see more clearly in forthcoming chapters, agency emerges in and through the construction of the person in his/her relations, where God is the totality of world and God's power/human power to act/be is the ambiguous power of that interrelated world of becoming.

Ontological Interrelatedness in Object Relations Theory

This section will briefly introduce ontological interrelatedness as it is understood in object relations theory, using primarily the work of W. R. D. Fairbairn and later feminist revisions. Object relations theory, a descendant of Freud's psychoanalysis, posits that persons, as personality,

72. Soelle, *Choosing Life*, 18.

psyche and behavior, develop in and of relation to others. The others are both "real" persons in the world, "external" to a particular person, and an "internalized" other in the world "internal" to a person. According to object relations theory there is no person or subject who is not constituted of her or his relations with others or objects, no person who exists outside of relations with others. Object relations theorists are not, like theologians, interested in the nature of *all* existence. They are rather interested in the specific "nature" of human psyches, their development, structure, function, and content. Our discussion assumes that object relations theorists, like all personality theorists, hold an implicit ontology that, though not explicitly theological, can be stated theologically. When Greenberg and Mitchell say of Fairbairn's theory, "The fundamental motivational force is understood to be the search for and establishment of relations with others,"[73] theologians might ask whether or not God can be spoken of as a "fundamental motivational force" and, if so, can God also be that which has us searching for and establishing relations with others. The above theological discussion posited God as the power of interrelatedness, the "organic restlessness" of the web which moves us in our becoming. This restlessness of the web which has us seeking and establishing relations is not to be understood as moving from unrelatedness to relatedness but moving toward maintaining and enriching relationship in order to live at all. I am suggesting that this can be understood as a "fundamental motivational force." With enough congruence in their respective ontologies, object relations theory can work in conjunction with a process/liberation theology, and bring to it a more detailed account of the internal or intrapsychic workings of the construction of human personhood.

Freud's psychoanalytic theory always assumed the presence of another.[74] The key to the psyche was to be found by exploring, through the relationship with the analyst, the early relations with others, usually parents. For Freud the relation with the other is a means to satisfying a biologically rooted drive, but for Fairbairn, and other object relations theorists, the relationship is not the means but the end.[75] According to

73. Greenberg and Mitchell, *Object Relations*, 177.
74. Ibid., 9.
75. Greenberg and Mitchell suggest two different models of object relations, the drive/structural (Freud) and the relational/structural (Fairbairn and others) which is clearly a descendent of Freud's but also a significantly different theory.

Fairbairn the fundamental need out of which the human psyche develops is the need for relationships with others, not the need to reduce the tension of unsatisfied biological drives, as it is in Freud. Fairbairn recalls the cry of a patient in his care, "You're always talking about my wanting this and that desire satisfied; but what I really want is a father." The core of human "being" is our desire for satisfying relationships with other. Outside of relationship, a child, or an adult, cannot survive nor can she/he thrive without a certain quality of relationship. "[T]he greatest need of a child is to obtain conclusive assurance (a) that he [sic] is genuinely loved as a person by his [sic] parents, and (b) that his [sic] parents genuinely accept his [sic] love."[76] It is from this core significance of human relationship that human beings live and move.

These relationships, which are the basic motivation for human behavior, are also constitutive of our psyches. Relationships are not only external, between two persons in the world external to a person's psyche, they are internalized such that relations with others constitute human psychic structure. The above statements must not be construed to mean that there exists a fully developed "person" who then seeks relationships. It is rather that being in relationship is part and parcel of being human. As Fairbarin states, "it is impossible to gain any adequate conception of the nature of an individual organism if it is considered apart from its relationships to its natural objects; for it is only in its relationships to these objects that its true nature is displayed." Loomer suggested that our understanding of a thing must be sought in the thing itself and its relationships. Fairbairn seems to be following this same maxim, although he is seeking understanding of the person and relationships as they develop internally. Ego is always attached to objects, which are in a sense "mental representations"[77] of actual external persons in relationship. There is no unrelated ego or an ego that is separate from its object relations, so the structure and content of the psyche is that of relationship, ego and object. Therefore we are constructed of relationships internalized such that we are our relations with others. Jean Baker Miller and others at the Stone Center speak of a "being-in-relationship" that develops into a "self-in-relationship"[78] not as one who begins separate

---

76. Fairbairn, *Psychoanalytic Studies*, 39.
77. Greenberg and Mitchell, *Object Relations*, 10–11.
78. Jordan, *Women's Growth in Connection*.

and then attaches to another but one whose being is always and only "in relationship." Loomer spoke of "mutual internal" relations in which and through which we constitute each other.

Human personhood develops through relatedness and through changing forms of relationship. According to Fairbairn we develop from the complete dependence of infancy through a "transitional stage" to the "mature dependence" of adulthood.[79] There is never a time when we are "independent" in the sense of existing apart from our dependence on our internal/external relations with others. The development of human personhood develops in the shifting landscape of relations internalized, repressed, and revised in light of relations with external others, a process we will explore in detail in the next chapter. Loomer suggests that theologically we're not interdependent because we love one another but that we love because we are interdependent.[80] We seek relationships not so that we will become interrelated but because we are already interrelated and our very life, our ego/self existence, depends on maintaining that relatedness. Interrelatedness is the nature of our existence and more relatedness is the goal of our growth.

For Loomer interrelateness is primary and "becoming" is ultimate. Fairbairn too presents a model of dynamic interrelatedness, describing that which structures the human psyche as dynamic structure where energy and structure are inseparable.

> The inert and indivisible particles or atoms, of which the physical universe was formerly thought to be composed, are now known to be structures of the greatest complexity embodying almost incredible quantities of energy—energy in the absence of which the structure themselves would be unintelligible, but which is equally difficult to explain in the absence of the structures.[81]

The ego then is energy or event. There are no structures into which a separate energy is imparted. The relations of which we are made are dynamic structures, moving energy out of which patterned configurations appear but which are never fixed substances or containers. Object relations theory assists us in thinking of the event, or actual occasions of experience, as internalized or held in endopsychic structures wheth-

---

79. Fairbairn, *Psychoanalytic Studies*, 145–46.
80. Loomer, "Size of God," 33–34.
81. Fairbairn, *Psychoanalytic Studies*, 127.

er conscious or unconscious. In terms of human personhood then we are once again moving toward an image of a person as constituted of energy that moves through time and space in a web of interrelatedness; and now we add, an energy of interrelatedness that moves to constitute our external and internal "being."

Feminist appropriations of object relations theory have pointed out that while object relations theory has always assumed the presence of a "real" person external to the developing subject, the focus has been on the impact and development of a *subject* who relates to and internalizes an *object*. If interrelatedness permeates, sustains, and creates human personhood in the way suggested here, then we must also attend to the subjectivity of the object. In the relationship both subjects are affected. Jessica Benjamin calls this the "intersubjective view" of human development. "The intersubjective view maintains that the individual grows in and through relationship to other subjects. Most important, this perspective observes that the other whom the self meets is also a self, a subject in his or her own right."[82] Benjamin goes on to point out that we need the tension of focusing on the intersubjective field between subjects as well as the "intrapsychic" world internal to a subject which is constructed of internalized relations. The lines between the intersubjective and intrapsychic are murky, thus the need to attend to how one impacts the other.

Cultural arrangements, structures of power and social location as well as their coextensive symbol systems, will impact the form and content of the internal object relations that Fairbairn and others postulate as our constitutive psychic elements. In object relations theory feminist revisionists have found a compatible concern for relationality, but extend the purview to include the manner by which culture sets the route for internalized object relations. In the web of interrelatedness in which we live and move and have our being culture is an inseparable influence on the relationships of which we are made. For instance, object relations theorists focus on the infant-mother relationship which cannot be considered apart from the culture of roles, for one, assigned to mothers. Those cultural prescriptions for what it means to mother, how one should mother and the way by which mothering assigns women a position, will inevitably form the content and dynamic character of the

---

82. Benjamin, *Bonds of Love*, 19–20.

relationship and therefore the content and character of the internalized object relations. Culture, of course, operates in the same dynamic web, creating and being created by persons who have been created by the occasions of past cultural experiences. Object relations theory aids us in conceptualizing persons as essentially relational, not as selves who become related, but as subjects who are made of our dynamic internal/external relations. Poststructuralist feminist theory picks up this question of culture, posits an ontology of interrelatedness, and focuses on the procedures of culture in the dynamics of human subjectivity.

Ontology in Butler's Poststructuralist Feminist Theory

Butler's poststructuralist feminist theory offers a direction for conceptualizing persons as radically culturally constructed. Before plunging into a discussion of what I argue is a posited ontology of interrelatedness in Butler's theory, it is necessary to briefly address the question of whether or not one can speak of such a thing as an "ontology" in poststructuralist "theory" which some would argue is no theory at all.[83] Poststrucutralist thinking suggests that all categories of thought expressed in language and discourse are open to interrogation. Nothing should be taken for granted or assumed. Furthermore, that which is posed as "clearly" assumable is itself a construction of discourse, and therefore an act of power making that which is arguable appear unarguable. Poststructuralism suggests that all categories, all ontological assumptions, are open for contest and that in fact we should look to the way in which those assumptions have been constructed for use by the ruling hegemonies. Butler explains her position thus:

> [I]f there is a point, and a fine point, to what I perhaps better understand as postructuralism, it is that power pervades the very conceptual apparatus that seek to negotiate its terms, including the subject position of the critic; and further, that this implication of the terms of criticism in the field of power is not the advent of a nihilistic relativism incapable of furnishing norms, but rather, the very precondition of a politically engaged critique. To establish norms that are beyond power or force is itself a powerful and forceful conceptual practice that sublimates, disguises

---

83. For discussions about poststructuralism as theory, see Butler, "Contingent Foundations"; Butler and Scott, *Feminists Theorize the Political*; and Weedon, *Feminist Practice*.

> and extends its own power play through recourse to tropes of normative universality. And the point is not to do away with foundations, or even to champion a position that goes under the name of antifoundationalism....
>
> It seems that theory posits foundations incessantly, and forms implicit metaphysical commitments as a matter of course, even when it seeks to guard against it; foundations function as the unquestioned and the unquestionable within any theory. And yet, are these 'foundations', that is, those premises that function as authorizing grounds, are they themselves not constituted through exclusions which, taken into account, expose the foundational premise as a contingent and contestable presumption.[84]

An ontology as that which is the "nature" of reality or of being itself, when posed as a fixed given, works to keep in power those who define reality. Feminists have argued, for instance, that to contest an ontology of a stable and autonomous subject is to negate the possibility of politics, which in and of itself implies that we must accept the rules for what counts as a basis for politics. Poststructuralism does not necessarily mean that we must refuse any ontological position but it does mean that we must look into the dynamics of power at work in establishing a position and open that position up for the possibility of refusal or revision. An ontological position, consciously contingently and temporarily posited, is one that allows for and encourages further contestation. I am arguing that while Butler's poststructuralist thought questions an ontology of essence and substance it does hold within it an alternative posited ontology of dynamic interrelatedness, perhaps not explicitly discussed in the same terms that I use but implied in the notion of a radically constructed subject.

To argue that human personhood is radically constructed is to say that person does not appear as an intact individual essence in neat coherent substantive form but rather is built, pieced together over time. We can think of Butler's work in terms of process thought as an excavation of the historical chain of actual occasions, the events of the past that have framed the present and will shape the future. The very idea of construction evokes an image of movement, of fitting and re-fitting, of changing structure and form until an effect of a whole is accomplished.

---

84. Butler, "Coningent Foundations," 6–7.

Butler argues that the site of this construction is culture, that human personhood is made in the context of culture that frames and shapes its structure, form and process. Human personhood is then constructed *in* culture and *by* culture. Butler suggests that to speak of a "person" presupposes a subject position, a linguistic category rather than an ontologically fixed entity. Persons are intelligible to the extent that they have been made intelligible by language and its regulatory practices. Language then is one, if not the primary, experience in the chain of occasions of experience that make a person. The person emerges in and is constituted of cultural matrices, not as an intact reflexive being who is then dropped into culture to be shaped and molded, acted upon by the power that be, but an effect of the culture of which the person is constituted, for which the person acts as representative, and against which the person resists. Identity and its categories, the definitions by which we understand ourselves and others to be persons at all, "are in fact the *effects* of institutions, practices, discourses with multiple and diffuse points of origin."[85]

Butler also argues that human personhood is constituted *of* culture. It could be that construction takes place as a fitting together of building blocks, which are each an immutable substance, then personhood would be a set of related substances. However, the thesis here argues that the "building blocks" of personhood are also culture. That constitutive pieces are the culture which is also the context in which the construction happens, suggests that personhood is not built of pieced together related substances. Culture is not substance, not fixed entity, but a dynamic construction itself, constituted of humanly constructed meanings, a "matrix" of discourse, practice, and institutions. The vision provoked is one of an organic web of moving relatedness in which no one thing, especially in this case person and culture but also the "elements" of culture, i.e. discourse, practice, and institutions, exists apart from the other.

This matrix or web of interrelated regulatory and creative agencies is not an intact structure that remains fixed across time but is a structure that gives the *appearance* of a coherent "entity" by virtue of the fact that the regulations or norms are "cited" and "reiterated" over time. Loomer's order emerges out of becomingness and Faribairn's

---

85. Butler, *Gender Trouble*, ix.

"endopsychic structures" are psychic energy. Loomer, Fairbairn and Butler each build on a notion of structure as energy, not as a container into which energy needed for movement is poured, but structure that is the energy itself moving in repeated patterns and functions. Butler's "materialization" of the subject is an effect of continual reiteration of norms until they appear "natural" and fixed rather than what they actually are, an emergent of an historical practice that is continuing even as it claims to be that which "is." "In other words, the 'coherence' and 'continuity' of 'the person' are not logical or analytic features of personhood, but, rather, socially instituted and maintained norms of intelligibility."[86] While the subject carries the appearance of coherence, that coherence is an effect of being constituted again and again, never complete, never finished, yet constructed in the norms of the "law" which over time have a "naturalized effect."[87] This process is historical, moving through a "temporal process"[88] in which the present is already implicated in and only made intelligible in light of the past. "Crucially, then, construction is neither a single act nor a causal process initiated by a subject and culminating in a set of fixed effects."[89] This continual reiteration of norms not only points to the constructed nature of presuppositions of the "natural," "universal" or "ontological," but the very necessity for reiteration suggests that the effect never fully takes, that there is a "constitutive instability"[90] indicated in the need for reiteration and therefore, in the constructive process which is the subject. The person is not constructed of substances but of reiterated discourse, ritualized practices, and historical chains of citation to previously cited laws of intelligibility that only have power because they continue to be cited. If these suddenly ceased the person would, in Butler's imaginary, cease to "be" or count as person at all. As we will see, it is this threat of "non-being" and its consequential instability in the subject that opens the possibility for revision and resistance and leads us to the site of agency.

This kind of constructivism has deep implications for thinking about bodily experience and the internal world of the psyche. I said at

---

86. Ibid., 17.
87. Butler, *Bodies That Matter*, 10.
88. Ibid.
89. Ibid.
90. Ibid., 10.

the outset that it would be necessary for a feminist theological anthropology grounded in the context of intimate partner violence to be able to identify the person as mind/body. Butler's notion of radical construction suggests that the body "materializes" in construction, once again a process that must not escape our interrogation. To question the body, to argue its construction in discourse, and to look after that of which it is constructed, is not to say that there is no body but rather to rethink the category of "body," to subject "body" to critical inquiry, especially that of body that is assumed as fixed. Butler's schema questions the ontology of mind/body dualism to the extent of questioning the existence of any pre-discursive or pre-cultural distinction. This is not to say that the biological does not exist but rather to question the appeal to the irreducibility of body. We eat; we sleep; we breathe and yet that which constitutes eating, sleeping, breathing is, as we know, open for debate. In light of poststructuralist interrogations, the mind/body distinction becomes unsustainable, as does the distinction between a person's internal and external world. Congruent with, I believe, but also the pushing the edge of, object relations theory, Butler questions the distinction in the subject of internal/external. If psychic structures are made of internalized object relations then we cannot presume a subject who performs an internalization because we would be referring to a subject who, according to our own theory, does not exist until the internalization is made. The subject comes into being in the process of internalization. The internalization, as the energy of psychic structures rooted in relationship, and externalization, as the practice of reiteration and re-enaction of those internalized relations, suggests a process by which the internal and external make each other in a continual process of regulated construction. As Butler states, "What constitutes through division the 'inner' and 'outer' worlds of the subject is a border and boundary tenuously maintained for the purposes of social regulations and control."[91] That which appears external reemerges as the internal projected and/or reiterated in service of the hegemony that benefits from the division. And yet, once again, in the instability inherent in the construction of internal/external, also resides the possibility and power of resistance to that very same hegemony. That which is repressed, the "constitutive outside," the unknown, unspoken, the exclusions made in any categori-

---

91. Butler, *Gender Trouble*, 133.

zation or identification, lingers beyond that which is acknowledged and assumed, threatening to appear in those minute spaces of incompletion to challenge the cited rules of personhood. Chapters 3 and 4 will pursue in more detail a discussion of the mutual constitution of mind/body/culture and construction as the necessary site of agency. The point I want to make here is that Butler's theory of construction holds a posited interrelatedness that finds enough congruence with the theologies and object relations theories presented above that we can proceed toward a theological anthropology such as the one I have suggested.

Return to Context

I have proposed a direction for a theological anthropology of human agency that suggests we can conceive of persons as made of energy operating in a web of interrelatedness. This constitutive interrelatedeness calls into question the categorical distinctions we make between mind and body, person and culture, and God and human, so that to speak of one is to speak of the other and the activity of one is activity in the other. As the energy and power of interrelatedness, God is identified with the totality of the world (and the cosmos) including the possibility of good or evil that suggests a fundamental ambiguity in the power of life. In order to understand human personhood we must then attend to the historical chain of events and the current intrapsychic and intersubjective context of relatedness. At every level and from every angle the need for sustained and enriched relationship is primary. If we are concerned with the possibility of an enriched web of relations, which by definition means more life and more subjectivity for all persons, then we must assess the character and structure of that interrelatedness for its use of power.

In the next chapter we will explore movement and development of this power of interrelateness in the construction of the intrapsychic and intersubjective spheres. However before moving on we should return to the context of intimate partner violence and ask of the fit between an ontology of interrelatedness and the propositions made above, and the concrete practice of care in light of intimate partner violence. At this point two areas seem important to examine for their significance to the context, the dynamics of human relationships and the nature of the God/human relations. The literature in intimate partner violence, reviewed in chapter one, contends that the primary dynamic of intimate partner violence is power and control wherein one person uses power to control the other. The literature also places the roots of this violence in the culture of patriarchal oppression and the objectification of women. From a perspective of interrelationship, this use of power in interpersonal and sociocultural contexts, radically shapes both the victim and the perpetrator of violence. This unilateral or hierarchical use of power works to give the appearance of freeing or increasing the stature of the one in control but ultimately diminishes both parties. While it might be said that the power of this kind of relationship is not relational power, the line of thinking posed above suggests that the power of the relationship *is* relational power to the extent that all power is relational power. It is the need for sustained relationship and the resultant fear of loss of that relatedness that might motivate the desperation for control. However, we cannot overlook the way that culture creates and gives structure to this dynamic. A historical and cultural analysis suggests that the use of power is gendered and supports a paradigm of domination by men over women. The cultural matrices of language and practice set the terms for what counts as strength or weakness, love or control, intimacy or abuse, and sex or violence. These terms are lived out in personal relationships and form human psychic development which means that both parties live in a dynamic that both creates and diminishes them. Resistance to the use of power for control is needed in order to move from a unilateral oppressive form of relational power to one that enriches and enlivens the web, or otherwise stated, in order for healing to happen. Concretely resistance will act to ensure the safety and on-going fullness of life for all persons and transform the sociocultural order for justice understood as right, or life giving, relations. The basis and character of the agency assumed in the call for resistance will be taken up in the next two chapters and is the crucial point of this volume.

    We need also to consider the implications of such an ontology as this for God/human relations. If relationship structured in power by control is the root of the problem in intimate partner violence then we must look at the "nature" of the God/human relationship for its complicity in or resistance to this dynamic. A non-responsive unambiguous wholly other God repeats the problem of unilateral power. A victim of intimate partner violence relating to a God to whom she must submit her will, to whom she must look for ultimate guidance, or upon whom she must rely suggests a God who operates very much like an abuser, and ultimately means diminishment of subjectivity and stature. The power of the God/human relationship by the criteria posed here lies in its mutual dependence and intersubjectivity. The activity of God as the restlessness of the web is also the activity of the person. This brings the focus to human agency, to the here and now of the world which in its wholeness is God. This God is ambiguous[92] and does not offer a clear set of rules by which to live, nor is it a persistent cause for good, but this God does give persons a reason to trust the web of life itself and can encourage resistance to that which diminishes life. God as the whole of the world suggests passionate attachment to concrete life that cannot transcend concrete experiences of fearful and broken bodies and spirits. The dynamic energy of the becomingness of interconnection suggests that this God holds the possibility for revision and change in any person or situation, and, of course, the possibility of further oppression.

---

92. The notion of ambiguity in the context of intimate partner violence has serious and complex implications which will be discussed in detail in chapter 4.

3

The Constructed Psyche

AT THE OUTSET OF THIS BOOK I SUGGESTED THAT A THEORY/THEOLOGY of human agency requires that we pose a cultural construction of persons that could keep central both body and psyche. My thesis is that agency arises from the deep cultural construction in and constitution of persons. This chapter begins the discussion of the process by which persons are made as and of mind/body/culture in a way that keeps central both body and mind, and sets the basis for understanding human agency. While the previous chapter set the ontological and theological bases for thinking of persons as constructed in and of relationship, this chapter and the one following take up a more specific focus on the development, function, and content of that which makes a "person" in the web and power of relatedness. A posited ontology of constitutive dynamic interrelatedness holds deep implications for thinking about the nature and development of human personhood. It may be clear that life itself is coexistent with interrelatedness but exactly how does this relatedness work to make persons who are mutually constituted of mind/body/culture? This chapter inquires of the "nature" of the intrapsychic and intersubjective spheres. How do these spheres of energy, of becomingness operating through the principle of relatedness, create and operate in the structures of psyche and culture in, what we have come to define as, human personhood? Chapter four will continue this line of inquiry more specifically directed at the "nature" of the material, or the body, as related to the psyche and constructed by and constituted of culture.

The cultural, psychical, and material dynamics at work in intimate partner violence highlight the concrete significance of these somewhat abstract theoretical imaginings. As discussed in chapter one, discourse on intimate partner violence revolves around various foci including the social, as in the gendered and privatized organization of the family, cultural, including the normative meanings assigned to sex, violence, love, or woman, material, such as injury to bodies and socioeconomic ramifications, and psychological, with reference to aspects such as the motivations of perpetrators and victims or the effects of trauma. I am proposing in this book that the radical cultural construction and culturally constituted nature of human nature is one way to make sense of human personhood in light of the pastoral experience of caring for persons in the context of intimate partner violence. As the movement/field/discourse of intimate partner violence has expanded, competing claims related to cause, effect, and solution have been pronounced, and positions established, defended, and challenged.[1]

This chapter and the next open up within the field of intimate partner violence the discussion of cause and effect, which has little meaning in light of the depth of interrelatedness and mutual constitution here proposed. Theories of cause and effect assume a linear progression in which there is a final cause. Process metaphysics, as described in the previous chapter, and poststructuralist interrogation, call into question any final cause or linear progression. Under scrutiny any cause can be understood as effect and any effect as a cause; they constitute each other so that trying to pinpoint a final cause is at least futile, if not nonsensical. The literature in domestic violence does suggest that the dynamics of intimate partner violence are complex and "interdisciplinary." Although cause and effect is the concern of much of the literature, my concern is with the identifications made by the literature that can, I think, be understood as the multiple, complex and coextensive "elements" of human personhood that are at play in intimate partner violence. The idea that thinking of persons as constructed by and constituted of culture helps make sense of the "truths" of competing claims from various positions within the field is, of course, implied.

---

1. One of the debates within domestic violence discourse is the extent to which what was once a political movement, a descendant from the women's movement, has become a "field" which then requires institutions, experts, theories, not to mention funding. Which already established field is the most appropriate location for this burgeoning discourse, i.e. criminal justice, psychology, health care, politics, is thus also debated. For some of these discussions, see Ferraro, "Dance of Dependency"; Lamb, *New Visions of Victims*; G. Walker, *Family Violence*.

This chapter begins with the question of how it is that "spheres," such as intrapsychic and intersubjective, or cultural and psychological, can be spoken of as identifiable spheres when the very nature of the discussion calls into question the distinctiveness and boundaries of those areas. The chapter continues with a summary of Fairbairn's object relations theory of the psyche as constituted of relationships, and human development as development through forms of relatedness, which sets the groundwork for a theory of the cultural construction of the psyche. Following the summary of his position, contemporary object relations theorists will support an expansion of Fairbairn's theory in three areas: the multiplicity and ambiguity of the ego, the intersubjectivity of development, and the constitutive nature of culture. The concluding section will not only make connections between the psyche, theology, and intimate partner violence, but will also point toward an understanding of the body as part of this mutual construction, (psyche/culture becomes psyche/body/culture in chapter four) and a concept of agency as emergent from these constructions, to be taken up in chapter five.

Speaking in Categories

This chapter will explore the relationship of the internal and external, of nature and culture even as those very categories and the boundaries they establish are called into question. A poststructuralist perspective requires here at least a literary moment of reflection on the difficulty of speaking in established categories in order to deconstruct those very categories. It is one of the presumptions of this book that indeed we have nothing but established categories from which to speak and that those same categories may indeed be turned on themselves, so to speak, in order to expose their constructed nature, to deconstruct existing boundaries and then propose a temporary reconstruction. Contrary to Audre Lordes' battle cry that the master's tools cannot take down the master's house,[2] the master's tools are indeed the only tools we have. But we may be able to use them to build tools never previously imagined; therefore offering new tools built out of old pieces which can then be used once again to tear down and rebuild. The difficulty in using categories such as internal or intrapsychic and external or intersubjective, or subject and object, is that they appear to be discrete, and often

2. Lorde, "Master's Tools."

oppositional. This chapter speaks in these categorical terms even as I argue that the internal is made of the external and the external of the internal, that the subject/object relationship is always also an object/subject and subject/subject relationship. It is important and necessary to keep language that speaks to the differences in various spheres and perspectives. Questioning the basis upon which the category is established is not necessarily advocating for the negation of the category but may "free it up," as Butler says.[3] It remains necessary to speak of the inner world of a person, not in opposition to or separate from the external world, but more as an indication of position and perspective, the difference perhaps between figure and ground.

Another problem arises in this discussion related to the nature of the "real." There can be a tendency to speak of "reality" as that which is external to a person's psyche as opposed to the "constructed" reality that exists "all in your head." Likewise to speak of a "culturally constructed" body rather than a "natural" body can raise criticisms of negating the "realities" of bodily limitations. The constructed is mistakenly assumed to be that which is not real. But, as Butler asks, why is it that to speak of the constructed becomes equated with "artificial" or as something not real and therefore as that which is "dispensable," or at least not to be taken seriously.[4] To argue that reality is constructed, that psyche and body are made not given, does not necessarily lead to the conclusion that reality can be changed easily, nor does it necessarily lead to the conclusion that it cannot be changed at all. Construction does not deny the deep material and psychological impact of oppression on the lived experience of women. A culturally constructed body does not mean that we are to take any less seriously the scars on the bodies of battered women. A culturally constructed and constituted psyche does not relieve individuals of responsibility and accountability.

This very discussion raises the question of what regulations are operating that make it necessary to "defend" constructed reality as "reality." Who and what is served by the establishment and maintenance of boundaries between what is and is not constructed, often posed as "natural" versus "cultural," "internal" versus "external" or "nature" versus "nurture"? As Butler states, "What constitutes through division the

---

3. Butler, "Contingent Foundations."
4. Butler, *Bodies That Matter*, xi.

'inner' and 'outer' worlds of the subject is a border and boundary tenuously maintained for the purposes of social regulation and control."[5] A culturally constructed psyche/body threatens the power of those who use the distinctions in order to argue for that which cannot be changed at all or must be changed within an *individual* as opposed to within the whole system of sociocultural practices, discourses, and institutions. For instance, to argue in the context of intimate partner violence for the cultural construction and mutual constitution of psyche/body/culture raises challenges for discussions around not only the "nature" of men and women, especially in terms of aggression and passivity, but also responsibility, treatment, and perception of violence.

This project is rooted in the proposal that we are made up of all these constructs, culture, psyche, and body, that they are mutually constitutive of who we are as human persons. The dynamics of intimate partner violence direct us to the complexities and ambiguities of what it means to be persons at all. Herman revives a study of Holocaust survivors reminding us that while most in the study "complained 'I am now a different person,' the most severely harmed stated simply, 'I am not a person.'"[6] How is it that culture/psyche/body can make us or break us as persons? How is it that they work to make each other? The following sections in this chapter will explore one possible conceptualization of the process in a way that honors what we have learned from our attempts to care for human suffering in the context of violence in intimate relationships.

Object Relations Theory

In the previous chapter I suggested that Fairbairn's theory of "endopsychic structure" shared with Loomer's process theology, Soelle's liberation theology, and Butler's poststructuralism an ontology of dynamic interrelatedness in which the psyche develops out of a fundamental need for relatedness. I briefly addressed Fairbairn's understanding of developing structures of the psyche and motivation for human behavior as relational energy directed toward the search for and maintenance of relationship. From the perspective of the "internal," that part of human personhood that feels or appears to be internal to an individual,

5. Butler, *Gender Trouble*, 133.
6. Herman, *Trauma and Recovery*, 94.

Fairbairn provides a model for thinking about how it is that the psyche develops and, with some extension via feminist and other contemporary theory, can provide a basis for understanding the person as constituted of mind/body/culture. It is not enough to say that these three are related for we must also ask exactly how it is that they, which have been seen as related but distinct, make each other and also how this making finds congruence with what is learned through care of persons as victims and perpetrators of intimate partner violence. Psychoanalytical theorist Stephen Mitchell states, "Mind has been redefined from a set of predetermined structures emerging from inside an individual organism to transactional patterns and internal structures derived from an interactive, interpersonal field."[7] Fairbairn's, and others,' theories of object relations lead to a definition of mind or psyche, such as Mitchell's, which directs us to look at the development of psyche as constructed in a field, or web, of interactions or movements between persons who are mind/body subjects. The field includes feelings, actions, ideas, symbols, practices, institutions, persons, and, I would add, a host of things, creatures, geographies and earth rhythms. This section will explore the specificity of psychical development through object relations as a way to clarify the process by which the psyche is constructed in and constituted of culture.

Fairbairn based much of his theory of object relations on his clinical work with trauma victims who were soldiers with what he called the "war neurosis" and abused children.[8] He wondered what it was that made abused children want to stay with their abusive parents. Fairbairn concluded that this dynamic could be understood as the logical outcome of a child whose primary motivation was the maintenance of relationship at all costs. The essential force behind human psychological development is the "individual in his libidinal capacity"[9] of object seeking, not Freud's biologically based impulse or drive that requires tension reduction, nor his dual instincts of eros and thanatos, but one force or energy, that of interrelatedness.[10] All the structures of the psyche

---

7. Mitchell, *Relational Concepts*, 17.

8. See several of the essays in Fairbairn, *Psychoanalytic Studies*. For biographical background on Fairbairn see the introductions in Scharff and Birtles, *From Instinct to Self*; Skolnick and Scharff, *Fairbarin*; and Sutherland, *Fairbairn's Journey*.

9. Fairbairn, "Replies."

10. Fairbairn, "Libido Theory Re-Evaluated."

emerge out of the power of the libido operating towards its goal of more relationship between the ego and its others. There is, for Fairbairn, at the core of human personhood, not a biological essence, but an energy, libido, that is, by virtue of being energy, in constant motion, moving through relationship between a subject and an object, holding these relationships in certain patterned motions that under repetition appear as structures within the psyche. In the theological language of the previous chapter, the libido can be considered the becomingness that operates through a primary principle of relatedness, where the libido is ultimate or as Fairbairn calls it, the one "life instinct."[11] But how exactly does this object oriented libido structure the psyche as internal relations?

Fairbairn proposed a model of psychic structure that includes three relational structures that have different modes of relating, the central ego attached to the ideal object, the libidinal ego attached to the exciting object, and the anti-libidinal ego attached to the rejecting object.[12] Human subjectivity is constituted of internal ego/object relations that are representations of interactions between self and other. In the beginning, according to Fairbairn, there is ego, unitary and whole, made of the libidinal energy of relatedness seeking more relatedness to others. From the beginning the frustration of this libidinal energy also occurs when others, for all sorts of reasons that we will explore later, do not respond as expected or hoped for. In response to this rejection and the ego's anxiety over separation, which in essence is anxiety over death since life itself is relatedness and total separation would mean death, the others are then internalized through identification and introjection as objects.

Objects are internal structures, albeit internal structures that emerge in the interactions of prior internal structures with prior external structures. "An internal object may be defined as an endopsychic structure other than an ego-structure, with which an ego-structure has a relationship comparable to a relationship with a person in external reality."[13] The object is not a person per se but representative of "emotionally significant aspects of persons" upon whom the person depends. An infant comes into the world completely dependent upon others to

11. Ibid., 115–56.

12. Fairbairn's terminology for these structures changed over the years. These are the terms he finally used beginning in Fairbairn, "Nature of Hysterical States."

13. Fairbairn, "In Defence of Object Relations Theory."

care for her or his survival needs. The infant experiences those interactions with certain affective responses, largely determined in the earliest phase by whether or not the need for the other is satisfied. There are people and things all around that respond to the baby and to whom the baby responds. The internal relationship of ego to its objects are "comparable with those in which the personality as a whole participates in the world of outer reality; but the form which they assume remains conferred upon them by the child's experience of situations and relationships in the earliest years of life."[14] The infant internalizes his or her perception of the interactions between the infant and the world around him or her, not of course the actual other or the actual other's self experience although certainly those impact the former.

As the subjective experience of the infant in interaction with the world around her or him is introjected into her/his psyche, the interaction becomes the origin of an object relation. The object does not exist outside of the internal relation to the ego, and I suggest, the ego does not exist outside of its object relations. Persons live in "two worlds" at once, the world of inner reality and the world of external reality, the world of the unconscious and the conscious, the past and the present. For Fairbairn, Freud's distinction between the unconscious and the conscious is less important than the distinction between the two worlds of inner and outer reality,[15] or perhaps more accurately stated as the *perceptions* of inner and outer reality. The conscious and the unconscious of a subject are constituted of object relations that are portions of relationships between two subjects. This is a process that in fact proposes that the external and the internal make each other. "I" am made of and by my relations with others. The persons interacting in violent intimate relationships may also be seen as living in "two worlds," or perhaps multiple worlds (a possibility to be explored later in the chapter) the world of what is happening between and around them and the world of what is going on inside each of them, including the worlds of the conscious and the unconscious. The victim and the perpetrator each are made of a whole history of relations internalized to constitute who they are, how they feel, think and act and, I will suggest, are continuing to be made of the on-going relations in which they participate, including the violent

14. Fairbairn, "Experimental Aspects of Psychoanalysis."
15. Ibid.

one they are currently engaged in. In a sense what looks like a dynamic between two individuals may be described as a multilayered interaction between a host of relationships represented through a variety of forms and practices in the internal/external world of the two.

External relations are the basis for the content and form of the psyche; but we are still left with the question of why and how introjection happens whereby object relations are configured in the psyche. Fairbairn insisted that the introjection of an object is rooted in the dissatisfaction or frustration of relations that present both the possibility of more relation and of none. Given that relationship is absolutely necessary for life itself, for survival, and that no relationship means death, human beings are plagued with the anxiety of separation rooted in our fear of death. It is from this depth of fear that both victims and perpetrators can be heard to express anxiety over being alone. Separation anxiety should not be understood as a second fundamental force, as in the two instincts of life and death, but rather the fear of separation is a derivation of the primary energy of interrelatedness. Loomer's words come to mind reminding us that we love because of the power of interrelatedness, not the other way around. It can also be said that we fear because of the power of interrelatedness. Pure separation in life is not possible since life, by necessity, requires relatedness, but the strength of that reality is also what scares us whenever relatedness appears threatened. Thus "the incorporation or introjection of a representative of the original object is a purposive activity motivated by the need to make external reality appear more tolerable."[16]

The external is made tolerable by what Fairbairn calls the "moral defense."[17] The object is introjected or internalized when the other in some way fails the libidinal energy, which is the search and need for more relatedness. When the mother fails, from the infants' perspective, to be completely satisfying, which all mothers inevitably are, the child deals with this failure by internalizing her as object.[18] Introjection, by which an external other becomes an internal object in relation to sub-

---

16. Fairbairn, "In Defence of Object Relations Theory," 117.
17. Fairbairn, *Psychoanalytic Studies*, 66.
18. Fairbairn refers to this other as "mother" but there is no need to limit his theory here. It could be mother or father or anyone who is present in the infant's life. Although it must be conceded that the quantity of interactions the infant has with an "other" directly impacts the significance of her/his object relations.

ject, is therefore a defense against the threat of separation. The object is attached to the ego as a way to gain control over and keep the relationship. If you will not respond to me, give me love and receive my love, then I will make you a part of me. Fairbairn describes this process from the perspective of an abused child:

> If the delinquent child is reluctant to admit that his parents are bad objects,[19] he by no means displays equal reluctance to admit that he himself is bad. It becomes obvious, therefore, that the child would rather be bad himself than have bad objects; and accordingly we have some justification for surmising that one of his motives in becoming bad is to make his objects 'good'. In becoming bad he is really taking upon himself the burden of badness which appears to reside in his objects. By this means he seeks to purge them of their badness; and in proportion as he succeeds in doing so, he is rewarded by that sense of security which an environment of good objects is, of course, the same thing as to say that he internalizes bad objects.[20]

Later Fairbairn used theological language to describe the reason for the defense, saying that it is better to be a sinner in a world ruled by God where though I may be bad the world around me is good and there is hope for redemption, than in a world ruled by the Devil where one cannot escape badness and there is only the possibility of "death and destruction."[21] For a battered woman this internal defense might have her see herself as "bad" or at fault instead of the batterer or society because then there may be hope for change, but if violence and "badness" is all there is then what hope is there?

It is easier for one to accept one's own moral or "conditional" badness because one may be able to change that; but it is not easy to accept the rejection of others upon whom one depends. It seems impossible to change the other but if it is me who is "bad," unloving and unloveable, then I am in control. I can respond to the threat of loss of relationship by making the relationship a part of who *I* am. This act of aggression,

---

19. In his earlier work Fairbairn described the original object of introjection as a "bad" or "unsatisfying" object. He later revised this language to better reflect his meaning by saying that the original object is "pre-ambivalent" and "neither good nor bad, but in some measure unsatisfying," and which is only differentiated in its good parts and bad parts after the introjection. Fairbairn, "Nature of Hysterical States," 16.

20. Fairbairn, *Psychoanalytic Studies*, 65.

21. Ibid., 67.

the introjection of the object, is an attempt to defend against the threat of death. Control of a relationship is, then, a means by which to hold on to it. To speak of "badness" and control in this context should be read carefully. First "badness" is not necessarily a moral judgment about the quality of parenting, although we might come to that conclusion in the context of abusive parents, but is instead a subjective experience of the child's. Likewise "control" in this context is not necessarily a conscious intention to harm an other, for the sake of seeing him or her suffer, but rather a means of survival, by taking control of that which is threatening. Control in this case means making the relationship tolerable, but this control can be acted out as either coercion or submission.

It may be that some of the dynamics of intimate partner violence are techniques of dealing with internal object relations, control of relationship as defense against a threat or perceived threat, but in the context of a child's defense the terms of discussion about the power of interrelatedness used for control seem to shift, at least slightly. Children, in response to that which threatens survival and against which a child feels powerless, try to gain the power needed to have an impact. One way to gain that power and to make any change in the situation is to control the relationship by internalizing it. This internal dynamic mirrors (not to be understood as causes) the dynamic at play when a batterer uses power to control or coerce another, and, as I stated in the previous chapter, may then be understood as a way to hold on to relationship. The literature suggests that batterers may feel helpless or threatened, or that they feel their sense of entitlement as intense need. Victims may blame self and/or try to change the relationship by controlling their own behavior, being careful not to trigger episodes of violence, or controlling you through me. These feelings begin to make sense, which is not to say that they should remain unchallenged, if thought of in terms of internal object relations. Later in the chapter the techniques by which adults play out internal childhood dynamics and the way that culture structures these dynamics will add to this discussion, but here in the very basics of Fairbairn's theory appears one way of beginning to make psychological sense of power and control in relationships.

Internalization is the first step in Fairbairn's complex drama of relations, some of which remains conscious and some unconscious. The object is internalized through cathexis to the ego. The original internalized object is whole or "pre-ambivalent," representing at the same time the aspects of the mother that are satisfying and those that are unsatisfying; but under the pressure of holding both the satisfying and unsatisfying and the anxiety provoked by the possibility of separation, the unsatisfying object is split off and repressed. Fairbairn continues his description of the abused child's dilemma:

> The sense of outer security resulting from this process of internalization is, however, liable to be seriously compromised by the resulting presence within him of internalized bad objects. Outer security is thus purchased at the price of inner security; and his ego is henceforth left at the mercy of a band of internal fifth columnists or persecutors, against which defences have to be, first hastily erected, and later laboriously consolidated.
>
> The earliest form of defence resorted to by the developing ego in a desperate attempt to deal with internalized bad objects is necessarily the simplest and most readily available, viz. repression. The bad objects are simply banished to the unconscious.[22]

The ambivalence that arises from both needing the object and finding the object intolerable because it is rejecting and therefore threatening to life itself, is too hard to bear for an infant with few emotional resources to draw on, and therefore that part of the object that has failed the infant is split off from the original, repressed and relegated to the unconscious. This is of course only a temporary solution, since the object has not gone away, but simply works its power outside of the realm of awareness. An infant cannot reject "bad" parents upon whom he or she depends for life itself. In fact to the extent that the parents may be neglectful or "bad" the infant needs them, or someone, even more.[23]

The abused child, in addition to attachment to an abusing parent, also exhibits guilt and shame, the result of additional acts of splitting and repression. The object that has been internalized as a defense against unsatisfying relationship has aspects that are both "good" and "bad." The ambivalence that arises from the internal object which is both wanted and yet frustrating in its lack of being available, is too much to bear; thus the aspect of the object that is "exciting" is repressed

22. Fairbairn, "Nature of Hysterical States," 65.

23. It should be noted that the terminology of "bad" or "good" objects reflects the infant's subjective experience and is not a value judgment on parenting. Even the best of parents, as deemed so by the current cultural parenting values, will not completely satisfy an infant all the time, nor might we suggest, should they as will be discussed in the later section of this chapter on intersubjectivity.

and with it is sent the aspect of the object that is "frustrating," while the remaining "good enough" object remains cathected to the central ego. The representations of the object as that which is wanted for connection and the exchange of love, yet unreachable, and that which is rejecting, unresponsive to the child's needs, yet loved, are held in the unconscious as means to deal with the pain of ambivalence. They now reside together in the unconscious, the outcome of one "impulse"—the need for relationship, or otherwise stated as the power of interrelatedness.

Until now I have spoken of repressed objects as if they alone constitute the unconscious. But there are no objects without ego structures attached to them. Objects only appear cathected to the ego. The unconscious is actually made up of object *relations* which are ego and object. The ego identifies with, through introjection, an object that is in some measure both satisfying and unsatisfying. Fairbairn calls this primary ego structure, the "central ego" and its "ideal object." When the "bad" object is split off from the ideal object some of the "nucleus" of that object remains as the ideal object attached to the central ego. The central ego is the primary dynamic structure of the "I," the observer, situated in the conscious or preconscious present, constituted of libidinal (relational) energy, from which all other psychic structures originate.

The split off exciting object and rejecting object were a part of the ideal object that was wholly cathected to the central ego so the ego must also split, for where there is object there also must be ego. The libidinal ego is that portion of the ego that is wildly excited about relationship, not oriented toward the reality of the situation, but wants connection at any cost, going after what it wants and needs. On the other hand the anti-libidinal ego is that aspect that has been stung by rejection and deprivation and so pulls away, not willing to risk further harm. The portion of the central ego attached to the rejecting object is the aspect of the ego that is characterized by frustration and its antecedent, aggression, thus in his earlier work Fairbairn called this the "internal saboteur"[24] and later renamed it the "anti-libidinal ego."[25] This "internal saboteur" or the anti-libidinal ego "has aims inherently hostile to those of the libidinal ego in its alliance with the exciting object."[26] The libidinal ego, the por-

---

24. Fairbairn, *Psychoanalytic Studies*.
25. Fairbairn, "Experimental Aspects of Psychoanalysis," 74.
26. Fairbairn, "Nature of Hysterical States," 17.

tion of the central ego that is attached to the exciting object, is subjected to a "sustained aggressive and persecutory attack" by the anitlibidnal ego.[27] The rejection of the other is turned inward thus giving rise, by virtue of the antilibinal ego in its conflict with the libidinal ego, to guilt. Thus Fairbairn's model establishes three ego structures the conscious or preconscious central ego attached to its ideal object, the anti-libidnal ego attached to the rejecting object and the libidinal ego attached to the exciting object which are both by virtue of the central ego's repression held in the unconscious.[28] As the energy of the unconscious, these object relations may not be available to the child's awareness but are powerful sources of and motivations for all kinds of feelings, thoughts, and behaviors.

A narrative of this psychical drama as told from the subject position could proceed thus: I come into the world, a dynamic structure of life energy moving through a web of interconnections, completely dependent on others for life itself. I myself am a structure of energy that continues to move, change and develop through relations with others. Others both provide for me and sometimes fail to provide for me, give relationship and withhold relationship. If they withhold too much I will cease to exist. The pain of rejection is great because I need relationship for life. I cannot bear the possibility of death, so in the face of an other who is both satisfying my needs and frustrating me by failing to satisfy, at least as I perceive satisfaction, I take in the other as a part of myself. If I make the other me then I can hold on to the relationship; I can control the relationship and maybe then there is a chance to live. But the pain of needing the other so much and being rejected by the other is too great and so I remove those aspects of myself/other from my awareness, deny them, disown them in a way and yet they remain as that which I have refused. My desperate need for others and my fear of rejection, moving toward and moving away, my goodness and my badness, keep engaging each other in a region of the unknown but put pressure on, or periodically slip through, the barrier acting out their conflict in my current interactions with others. I am then plagued with guilt or shame at my need for others and/or my aggression towards them.

27. Ibid.

28. These structures superficially resemble Freud's ego, id, and super-ego, however Fairbairn's theory of dynamic structure and centrality of object relations rather than drive make them constitutionally quite different.

Expanding Fairbairn

According to Fairbairn the psychic structures are dynamic energy, specifically the dynamic energy of libido that is fundamentally the energy of relatedness. Internal relations born out of relationships with external others take the form of six structures: the central ego and its ideal object, the libidinal ego and its exciting object, and the anti-libidnal ego and its rejecting object. Maintenance of relationship is the driving force behind human development and life itself. The derivative fear of separation, that would mean death, encourages the maintenance of relationship at all costs and provokes the tension between that which desires connection and that which needs protection from disconnection. Fairbairn's theory of object relations sets the stage for thinking about psyche as constructed by the power of interrelatedness and constituted of dynamic relations with others. However the thesis of this project rests on the premise that the psyche is constructed by and of culture. Chapter two argued that there is presumption of an ontological interrelatedness behind a theory of cultural construction, and behind Fairbairn's object relations theory, but as of yet I have not identified the means by which the power of interrelatedness as it works to construct the psyche, or internal object relations as they structure the content of the psyche, are to be understood as dynamics of culture. Contemporary theorists add a dimension to Fairbairn's thought that moves in that direction.

In order to proceed toward a conceptualization of persons as culturally constructed and constituted in a way that will lend itself toward thinking of agency as arising from that construction, Fairbairn's theory needs expansion in three areas. Fairbairn's notion of an original unitary ego requires closer scrutiny. If the ego is *always* object related then there is no original unrelated ego that then attaches to or internalizes an object, but rather the ego comes into "being" with the object as internalization happens. Then splitting, though rooted in ambivalence, may be understood as part and parcel of life and human psychic development. Second, although Fairbairn takes the position of the subject as she/he relates to objects/others, an intersubjective perspective takes into account the mutual formation of two subjects where the position of object is only a partial perspective, from the point of view of one subject, not both. Third, Fairbairn does not take into account the way that culture, its language, practices, and institutions, prescribes relationships and therefore determines the character and form of interactions that are the basis for internalized relations; however his theory of object relations does enable such a move.

The Origins and Nature of the Ego

The origins and nature of the ego is the first area of needed expansion in Fairbairn's theory. In order to argue that persons are radically constructed in and of culture, the ego cannot be an "original" entity that later becomes related, a point that I believe is not contrary to Fairbarin's theory but does require further elaboration. This section will expand on the nature of the ego as fundamentally the energy of relatedness, as developing fluidly and continuously, and as characterized by ambiguity and multiplicity. These aspects of the ego will be essential in order to understand agency as ambivalently arising from construction, a point to be developed in chapter five.

In the beginning of human personhood there is only the power of dynamic interrelatedness, energy moving through the web of relations. Structure, form, coherence, and entity/identity emerge as effects of these movements. Fairbairn refers to an ego that is present from birth and then becomes split, however his reference to an "original, inherent and unitary ego (the 'unmodified' ego)"[29] speaks more to his theory of splitting than to an original "unrelated" ego. For Fairbairn ego cannot be understood apart from libido as object relatedness or structure as only emergent from energy. For Fairbairn function and structure cannot be abstracted from each other, the ego structure can only *be* in the energy of its functionality. Likewise libido, as the name of that energy which constitutes ego function and therefore structure, *is* the energy or power of the ego. There is not an extra-libidinal container (ego) into which libido enters so that it may function, nor is there free floating energy (libido) looking for a structure through which to operate. Libido, understood as the power of object relatedness that both seeks and establishes object relations, ego and object, I suggest, always appear coextensively. We cannot conceive of one without the other.

Fairbairn describes his theoretical position as:

> characterized by four main conceptual formulations:—viz. (a) a theory of dynamic psychical structure, (b) a theory to the effect

---

29. Fairbairn, "Psychoanalytical Treatment," 75.

that libidinal activity is inherently and primarily object—seeking, (c) a resulting theory of libidinal development couched, not in terms of presumptive zonal dominance, but in terms of the quality of dependence, and (d) a theory of the personality couched exclusively in terms of internal object-relationships.[30]

The use of the term "object-seeking" could imply that there is an entity that sends out a signal of sorts that looks for an object to attach to; however, with a more careful reading it is clear that Fairbairn uses the term "object-seeking" as a counterpoint to Freud's "pleasure-seeking"[31] and not to imply an ego that seeks objects through libido and then becomes related when libido finds an object. If all four of Fairbairn's conceptualizations, referred to above, are kept in mind, it may be better stated that libidinal activity is inherently the activity of object relatedness. There are six structures in Fairbairn's model of the psyche (central ego, ideal object, libidinal ego, exciting object, anti-libidinal ego, rejecting object) and none of them is an ego without an object. In the beginning there is becomingness and interrelatedness, to return to theological language, or the libidinal energy of ego/object relations. The beginning of personhood is the energy of dynamic relatedness that operates in and through relationships that are external/internal. The infant is born into a world of movement and interaction that immediately begins to give structure to the internal/external world.

Human development proceeds in the dynamic of shifting object relations as they are internalized, split, repressed, integrated and/or re-integrated. The movement of libido is multidirectional moving out through relationship and onward through more complexity, but also toward more simplicity and inward, away from external others and toward internalized others. The development of human personhood in this mode does not move from complete dependence to independence but from "primary dependence" to "mature dependence,"[32] through different forms or qualities of dependence and relatedness. Unlike Freud and others who see development as a movement through stages and

---

30. Ibid., 74.

31. Fairbairn, *Psychoanalytic Studies*, 137; and Fairbairn, "Libido Theory Re-Evaluated."

32. See "A Revised Psychopathology of the Psychoses and Psychoneuroses," in Fairbairn, *Psychoanalytic Studies*.

pathology as fixation or "developmental arrest" in one stage or another,[33] Fairbairn suggests that development is a matter of techniques for dealing with object relations. As the infant develops, experiencing more and more interactions, the resultant internal object relations provide the strategies by which the child responds to others and acts in the world. As time continues the child has a larger pool of internal resources from which to draw upon in the face of new relations. Every child will have some central ego relations, libidinal ego relations, and anti-libidinal relations but the organization, fluidity or rigidity, of these internal object relations will vary.

Fairbairn, like many of his peers, believed that earlier object relations held more weight, so to speak, in development. They were more apt to be repressed and harder to release. This makes sense given the early infant's lack of interactive history; however, there is no reason in Fairbairn's theory to believe that the pattern for any particular person's development is fixed early on or that later interactions cannot have significant and lasting impact, both for good and for bad. Personality development must be seen as dynamic and on-going. This is certainly a theory of an historical construction of the human psyche; the present is a result of the past, however, the future cannot be predicted nor determined. It may be possible to reconstruct a chain of events that have lead to a present interaction but we cannot predict, given a certain past, what will happen in the future. As Stephen Mitchell states, "It may be that later difficulties in living are often *not* direct causal products of earlier deprivation and problems, but a complex combination of the impact of early experience and reactions to later stresses and conflicts."[34] Early trauma does not *necessarily* lead to later pathology. Mitchell describes studies that have shown that even children with extreme deprivation in early childhood do not necessarily develop pathology. He stresses the importance of the quality of relationships throughout life and suggests that the "severity of psychopathology reflects not so much the earliness of the problems, but their rigidity and pervasiveness."[35] An exploration of history can give some clues as to how present events are being shaped in familiar patterns. The psychological dynamics of intimate partner

---

33. See Mitchell, *Relational Concepts*, for a discussion of object relations and developmental arrest theories of pathology.

34. Ibid., 145.

35. Ibid., 148.

violence then would require attention to not only early relational dynamics and life experiences of the individual partners, but also the pervasive reiteration of certain relational structural patterns presently lived out in families and in culture. Furthermore, it is conceivable that adult trauma can completely reorganize one's psyche and may create new rigid patterns.

This theorization calls into question an assumption of a pre-social core self and poses new possibilities for thinking of human personhood as more ambiguous and fluid than coherent and solid. This challenges the notion that there is in every infant a certain ideal potential that with the "right" environment the child will grow up to be who she or he *really* is or was meant to be. Under this more predominant way of thinking, there is something that is pre-social that holds the "real" core of the person. Using spatial metaphors, as Mitchell points out, we tend to assign the "core" to a place deep within and then assume that we can "peel away" the layers of adaptations and accommodations and get to that more "authentic" place.[36] Mitchell goes on to propose an alternative that takes a more temporal and historical approach to subjectivity:

> But it seems more accurate and, I believe, more useful, to regard the self as a temporal rather than a spatial phenomenon. The self *is* nowhere: the self refers to the subjective organization of meanings a person creates as he or she moves through time, doing things, like having ideas and feelings, including some self-reflective ideas and feelings about oneself.
>
> If the self moves in time rather than exists in space, it has no core; but it has many different ways of operating.[37]

As a temporal process, subjectivity and human personhood develop patterns or techniques (Fairbairn) to live and interact with self, others, and things in the world. The patterns may over time and repetition appear as fixed, structural, and content driven.

Mitchell continues, "In speaking about authenticity and inauthenticity, the crucial difference lies not in the specific *content* of what I feel or do, but in the relationship between what I feel and do and the spontaneous configuration and flow of my experience at that point in *time*."[38]

---

36. See "True Selves," in Mitchell, *Relational Perspectives*, 9.
37. Ibid.
38. Ibid.

To be a self or person or subject is then much more ambiguous than we might think. Object relations are shifting and changing through all ages and stages of life such that a person can think, feel, and be one way at one point in time and then, over time and accumulated experience, be authentically entirely different at another point in time. This does not mean that there is no coherence or continuity, or no individuality. The evolution of a person is constructed of past and present object relations that are related to each other over time and in their relatedness we find strands of connection that link one to another. Once again these connections are discernible looking back but not predictive of the future. Individuality appears as unique convergences of a multitude of relations in any moment in time.

Fairbairn describes personality development as proceeding through changing forms of relatedness and suggests that pathology is rooted in the inability to let go of repressed early ties such that certain familiar modes of relating become primary and rigidly adhered to. His implication is that healthy development is a matter of being able to rework internal relations, to release from repression, to re-integrate, to accept the ambivalence and ambiguity of relations with others in their satisfying and frustrating qualities. Internal relations may be released from repression, not because we decide to release them but because that is what happens as the ego continues repressing. Repression is not something that happens once; it must be reiterated over and over again. Fairbairn's theory of splitting and repression suggests that development of personhood is active and fluid as relations move and shift, and as emerging subjects access different aspects of their internal selves in light of current relations with others. However this mode of appropriating Fairbairn's theory requires a close look at his use of introjection and splitting.

Fairbairn proposes that objects are introjected because they are "bad." However bad is not to be understood as a value judgment but as a subjective and libidinal response based on whether or not the object is wholly satisfying, which, in Fairbairn's terms, means wholly related, fully giving and receiving love. But we must remember that no object is ever *wholly* satisfying, in large part because the object is also a subject. Therefore it is more appropriate to think of internalization of a bad object as a process of what *is*, not as a deviation from what *might be* in a perfect world. To start from the ideal of perfection as non-ambiguous would then direct us to interpret internalization as a problem but if ambiguity is seen as a given, and necessary, then the internalization of an object who is ambiguous in the face of a subject's needs is simply a mode of responding to ambiguity, but not necessarily the result of a problem that must be rectified. The power of interrelatedness is ambiguous, full of the potential for satisfaction and frustration, to which we respond by internalizing, and splitting and repressing. Splitting and repression can also be seen as useful ways to respond to ambiguity when it threatens our sense of being related, which means it threatens our sense of being able to exist. Subjects, at our best, can internally move between aspects of our selves as internalized relations, can repress or reintegrate as needed. What Fairbairn calls "pathology" occurs when continual adherence to a certain mode, or rigidity sets in.

Jane Flax provides a helpful description of the value of a subjectivity constituted of multiple modes of relating. She looks at two modes of ordering subjectivities—schizoid and borderline—which prove to be problematic in their lack of fluidity and multiplicity.

> Each is an excessively imperfect attempt to solve problems many humans share—how to manage the multiplicity that different contexts require, how to feel and think (especially simultaneously) without destroying ourselves and others.
>
> Both forms of subjectivity exemplify some of the dangers and costs of the lack of fluidity. Schizoid subjectivity is unnecessarily rigid and compartmentalized. Borderline subjectivity is so fragmented and inconstant that fluidity cannot cohere into usable shapes or meanings. Schizoid and borderline persons suffer a common difficulty. Neither can experience *simultaneously* the *distinctiveness* of different aspects of subjectivity and their mutuality.[39]

The problem is not that the core self has been lost to or obscured by environmental traumas or that there is not enough solidified self but rather that the modes of configuring and operating through relations are limited and reiterated over time such that other modes seem unavailable. This becomes crucial in a theory of agency that does not reside in a core self but more in the availability of a range in modes of relating.

---

39. Flax, *Disputed Subjects*, 103.

Intersubjectivity

The second area for expansion of Fairbairn's theory lies in the necessity of a theory of intersubjectivity, implied by Fairbairn but not developed.[40] Liberating, healthy, subjectivity expanding, and stature increasing techniques for object relating can only be fully understood when the intersubjective perspective is held along with the intrapsychic. Object relations, from the stance of the intrapsychic, refer to an internalization made by a subject who looks to an other for satisfaction of relational need. The object, as a mental representation of the other, is usually thought of as that which is not subject. From the perspective of the intrapsychic posed above, the object, while derived from the infant's or subject's experience of another subject, is nevertheless only derivative of the other subject. The object is one subject's experience of another subject but cannot *be* the other subject in its entirety since that entirety is not available, even to the other subject. However, in a world of dynamic interrelatedness we must assume that the subjectivity of the other/object influences the object relations of the subject/child. Furthermore, I suggest, building upon Jessica Benjamin's work, that subjectivity emerges *only* in the mutual recognition of subjects. Thus a shift is required that looks at Fairbairn's object relations theory from the perspective of the intersubjective field.

Faribairn's statement that "the greatest need of a child is to obtain conclusive assurance (a) that he is genuinely loved as a person by his parents, and (b) that his parents genuinely accept his love"[41] implies that mutual recognition of subjectivity is crucial to human personhood. The need described here is one of receiving and giving by both parties. The parents recognize the child and give love, this love is taken in by the child. The child also needs to give love and have that love received which requires that she or he see the parent as another subject separate from him or herself. To be a subject is to be in a position to speak, think, feel, act and know. The child in this scenario is active, participating in relationship, and influencing the subjectivity of the parent. The parent

---

40. For similar arguments for the expansion of Fairbairn to more explicitly include intersubjectivity, see Mitchell, *Relational Concepts*; Scharff and Birtles, *From Instinct to Self*; and critique by Greenberg and Mitchell, *Object Relations*.

41. Fairbairn, *Psychoanalytic Studies*, 39.

must be able to not only give love (satisfaction of the child's libidinal needs) but also must be able to receive from the child.

Fairbairn sees the psyche in a constant tension between the urge toward mature dependence and the reluctance to abandon infantile dependence (as internalized object relations). Development is a movement from one kind of dependency to another, from primary identification and complete dependence (more receiving than giving) toward dependence with differentiation. Differentiation, in this case, means the mutual recognition of subjectivity and difference but not independence. One's perspective and position are different than the other's and yet derived from and dependent upon interaction with her or him. Mature dependence involves "co-operative" relationships.[42] Mature dependence requires mutual recognition, loving and being loved, understanding and being understood. As Benjaimin states, "we actually have a need to recognize the other as a separate person who is like us yet distinct."[43] We find pleasure and enjoyment in the other's difference, the not-me quality, the reality that the other's actions and responses are not wholly predictable or controllable. Subjectivity/self/personhood requires both being recognized as a subject and being able to recognize the subjectivity of others.

Intersubjectivity suggests that in order to be a person at all one must not only recognize self but also recognize other, and in order to recognize an other a person must recognize self. So subjectivity or personhood emerges in the act of mutual recognition which is "essentially mutual."[44] I become an "I" because I am recognized. According to Benjamin:

> A person comes to feel that "I am the doer who does, I am the author of my acts," by being with another person who recognizes her acts, her feelings, her intentions, her existence, her independence. Recognition is the essential response, the constant companion of assertion. The subject declares, "I am, I do," and then waits for the response, "You are, you have done." Recognition

---

42. Ibid., 145.
43. Benjamin, *Bonds of Love*, 23. "Separate" is used here not to mean disconnected but different.
44. Benjamin, *Like Subjects, Love Objects*.

is thus reflexive; it includes not only the other's confirming response, but also how we find ourselves in that response.[45]

But the "I" who acts should not be conceived as an "I" that pre-exists recognition instead "recognizing and being recognized" occur at the same time.[46] Subjectivity emerges *only* intersubjectively. There is no subject until one is recognized as such and recognizes the other as subject.

The paradox is that, while we continue to need this mutual recognition, we also fear it because it often requires of us to let go internalized object relations which initially came into being as a defense against losing relatedness. I stated earlier that no object is wholly satisfying largely because the object is also a subject. If a subject aims to be wholly satisfying as an object of another subject, her or his subjectivity will be diminished and ultimately destroyed. For instance, if a mother strives to meet every need of the child, to be constantly available for whatever the child wants she will eventually lose her self and her own subjectivity, her ability to recognize herself as distinct from the child. In this scenario the child too will lose subjectivity in as much as subjectivity depends upon mutual recognition. If the mother is *only* satisfying then there is no need to internalize an object, no development of psyche, no subject to recognize and love and therefore no subjectivity of the child. If there is to be one subject, there must be (at least) two. If relatedness, and therefore life, is to continue then several ambiguities must be held in tension. The need for relatedness demands neither too much satisfaction nor too little. Some relationship must be lost in order to have more relatedness. Mutual recognition requires that one is both subject and object and that relations are coextensively internal object relations and intersubjective.

A return to Loomer's definition of stature and the use of power for control can help clarify this picture of intersubjectivity. Stature, as the "volume of life" you can take in without losing your integrity,[47] requires both more relatedness and less relatedness. There is a point where more relatedness becomes less. Stature and enrichment of the web requires

---

45. Benjamin, *Bonds of Love*, 21.

46. Meyers, *Subjection and Subjectivity* makes this point as a revision to Benjamin in *Bonds of Love*. While Meyers perhaps states it stronger then Benjamin, it is consistent with Benjamin who I think clarifies this point some in Benjamin, *Like Subjects, Love Objects*.

47. Loomer, "Size of God."

that the power of dynamic interrelatedness be used for mutuality. Mutuality involves giving and receiving and the recognition of the other as a distinct, but not separate, subject. In mutuality there is a movement toward and away, holding on and letting go. In contrast to mutuality, control of the other uses the power of relatedness unidirectionally. One gives and the other receives. It may appear that one is subject while the other is object but upon closer scrutiny it becomes clear that both operate more as objects and less as subjects. Neither one really recognizes self, nor is recognized by the other, as a viable subject, able to influence and be influenced or to love and be loved. Relationships that are built on unilateral use of power, as in those of domestic violence, usually hang on a precarious balance of just enough recognition of mutual subjectivity in order to maintain life at a minimal level but ultimately this dynamic diminishes and destroys the subjectivity of both. Created by the ambiguity of difference as the other side of relatedness the tension must be held in order to sustain or increase stature and subjectivity. If we take in more and more and give nothing, we will lose our integrity, explode, so to speak, under the internal pressure and cease to exist. The energy will cease to hold a recognizable pattern or structure. Likewise if we give and give and receive nothing, we also lose our integrity, implode under external pressure. In either case the tension has not been held. We can see that the ideal of mutuality is born out of the reality of intersubjectivity, which requires at least two subjects in mutual recognition in order for there to be one. It will become clear as we progress that agency, as an aspect of subjectivity, increases in this ability to hold the tension and resistance arises as libido/life continuously and paradoxically insists on becoming.

Culture

The third way that Fairbairn's object relations theory needs expansion is in the exploration of cultural prescriptions for relationship. Relational interactions are infused with language, practices, and meanings that both reflect and create the cultural field in and through which relationships come to be. A parent's response to a baby's cry will be shaped by the culture's web of meaning. For instance, how a baby should be fed, held, talked to, or how a cry should be interpreted, and even the parent's own feeling states and cognitions are cultural constructions. The cultural content of relationship is not incidental to object relations it is the material of which relationships are made and therefore the constitutive material of the psyche. If the basic need of human development is the maintenance of relatedness then it is culture that determines the structure, modes and qualities of relationship, not a pre-relational biological drive. Furthermore, if the agency, as well as the content, of internalization, splitting and repression is the ontological necessity of dynamic interrelatedness, and if all relatedness is made of culture, then culture is also the constitutive "material" of human intrapsychic/intersubjective development. Of course, given an ontology of dynamic energy, rather than static matter, culture as "material" is not "a" thing or "an" entity but an energy of continually constructed and reiterated practices, structures, and symbol systems.

The previous chapter considered Butler's theory of cultural construction as it held an implicit ontology of interrelatedness. This section will, through the lens of Butler's theory, look more closely at the workings of culture in this constructive/constitutive process, particularly in its use of power for both limiting and creating subjects. Butler proposes that if we are to understand human persons we should think about the manner in which persons are constructed in, by and of culture. As an effect of culture that continually institutes and re-institutes the norms by which human life is lived, persons come to appear as coherent and cohesive entities but are kept alive, so to speak, by the reiteration of those norms. The continuity over time is the result of continual references to the past, of appeals to "what everyone knows" and the authoritative power these references have by virtue of the continual reference. Once again, a trace of the line from the present back to the past can reveal that what was once thought "natural" or ontological is now perhaps "proven" to be "environmental" or culturally constructed. Not only do we tend to forget that the lines, between for instance, natural/cultural, rape/sex or love/violence, were drawn elsewhere but that they were *drawn* at all. In fact, Butler reminds us, "forgetting" serves the agenda of the ruling privileged who draw the line such that the current structures of power remain.

Let us take an overly simplified (and laughable at many levels) illustration. If a child is routinely dressed in pink, given pink toys, and sleeps and plays in a room decorated in shades of pink that child quickly identifies with pink. Pink is a means to connection with mother who oohs, ahs and smiles when the child wears pink. Pink is associated with satisfying relationship to Mom. When the toddler reaches for the blue toy and Mom reaches for the pink, saying "Oh look not that ugly toy, here is a beautiful toy for you," blue is internalized and repressed as that which is associated with rejecting unsatisfying relations. Now the child internalizes pink as a preferred color. It is not that the child learns to like pink because of a system of rewards, although that is also happening, the child now is identified with pink. Later when someone suggests that she learned to like pink because of the rules of patriarchal oppression she may authentically respond, "But I really don't like blue. I *really* do like pink." But we must continue the analysis even further. The cultural rule that girls like pink pre-existed this mother/daughter interaction and in fact set the terms for the mother's subjectivity. If Mother was constructed in a culture that prescribes gender as a necessity for subjectivity, in other words, there are no subjects who are not gendered male or female, and uses the color pink as a means of establishing gender so that girls are identified by pink and boys by blue, then Mother's subjectivity, and thus the child's, depends upon the maintenance of this cultural norm. Furthermore, over time this very construction may be proclaimed "natural," a claim justified by its pervasiveness and the earliness of its appearance in children. The few who do not fit into this norm are proclaimed as pathological or deviant due perhaps to some problem in their genes or upbringing and every attempt will be made to rectify this sad situation. Intersubjectivity requires, as Benjamin says, "a shared reality." There must be culture, enough shared practice, language and meaning system so that recognition can occur. As a basis for subjectivity, and so personhood, the depth with which these cultural norms construct who we are becomes more clearly understood.

In order to be a person one must be recognized as a subject; one must hold in the sociocultural milieu a position that is acknowledged and responded to. There must be at least a minimal "shared reality," between two persons that enables them to communicate, to give and receive from each other. One does not count as "person" unless granted that status by attribution to a position or a place in society that is then occupied by what comes to be known as "person." The increase of subjectivity is the enlargement of that place, so that the subject holding that position generates more response from others and, since subjectivity grows in interaction, is more able to respond in multiple and fluid ways to others.

However, subjectivity is produced within the regulations of culture that limit modes of response. According to poststructuralism, we are subjected to many cultural discourses and fields of interaction that determine the meaning of our experience, primarily through language. Chris Weedon describes the process by which subjectivity is produced:

> As we acquire language, we learn to give voice—meaning—to our experience and to understand it according to particular ways of thinking, particular discourses, which pre-date our entry into language. These ways of thinking constitute our consciousness, and the positions with which we identify structure our sense of ourselves, our subjectivity. Having grown up within a particular system of meanings and values, which may well be contradictory, we may find ourselves resisting alternatives.[48]

Language pre-exists us as persons and sets the meanings of experience, defines who is and who is not. We live by a long history of reference to prior acts and meanings. And yet language does not exist outside of the speaker. Language is a human act that represents, and creates, both shared reality and conflicting interests.

As Weedon goes on to say, we learn that we occupy sites of conflicting discourses, subjected to contradiction that we have not caused and yet is *our* experience. For instance, if you are slapped because your partner perceives that you have flirted with someone else and the general consensus (of friends, family, and not to mention the images of romance on television, in literature, etc.) is that he did it because he *loves* you so much that he gets wildly jealous, you may feel the contradiction of an experience, being slapped, that both feels like love and doesn't. Furthermore, the "general consensus" holds in place a patriarchal system that allows slapping in some contexts, and of some "persons," and not in others. Enough "slapping" of the one without intervening response from others would call into question the "personhood," or the one's claim to position or status in society at all, thus disallow any naming of the contradictions or questioning of how the "slap" gets defined. "*Everyone* knows it's because he loves you, not because he wants to hurt you. He just can't control his passion for you." These kinds of events are

---

48. Weedon, *Feminist Practice*, 33.

not events that happen to an already formed person, who then accumulates the experience as an addition to his or her core self, but indeed form and constitute the person, including her or his feelings and the meanings attributed to them.

Benjamin's work suggests that these dynamics of object relations can illuminate the persistence of gendered domination and subordination,[49] as in the dynamics of intimate partner violence. Benjamin begins with the observation that domination is a "two-way process"[50] that requires at least two participants, victim and perpetrator, who are held in this dynamic of the control of one over the other. The power of domination works because it forms, or "converts" the subordinate into a "willing" participant. According to Benjamin the domination/subordination patterning of gendered relationship happens when the tension of intersubjectivity breaks down and splitting results. This splitting both reiterates and recreates the splits of culture in which the two sides of a split are set in opposition where one is devalued and the other idealized, seen, for example, in male/female, rationality/nurturance, public/private. Western culture's particular mode of splitting assigns men to the side that dominates by splitting off nurturance, dependency or "moving toward" and women to subordination by splitting off what Benjamin calls "self-assertion" and what I have referred to previously as "movement away." Recalling the previous discussion of the relationship of splitting to the need for relatedness, it becomes clear that the persistence of all parties' participation in a relationship of domination/subordination persists because of its tie to the deep need for relatedness, as Benjamin says it, "a twisting of the bonds of love."[51] "It is a reaction to the predicament of solitary confinement- being unable to get through to the other, or be gotten through to-which is our particularly modern form of bondage."[52]

In a culture that encourages the use of power for control, rather than mutuality, the stage is set intrapsychically and intersubjectively for intimate partner violence. Aggression, in Fairbairn's terms, is about maintaining relatedness and control, accomplished by internalization.

---

49. Benjamin, *Bonds of Love*.
50. Ibid., 5.
51. Ibid., 219.
52. Ibid., 83.

The identification of self with the relationship is a means by which to have some control and influence over the relationship. As the relationship, both ego and object, is split under the pressure of holding the ambiguity in tension, the modes of the split are determined by culture. The culture encourages the use of power for control, rather than for mutuality which would also require valuing ambiguity, and hierarchicalizes and genderizes the resultant split. The perpetrator identifies in the split with control of the relationship through force and coercion. The victim identifies with control through nurturance, or by conforming her needs to the needs of the other.[53] If underlying this dynamic of control is the fundamental need for relatedness then we might understand to some degree how a batterer can feel entitlement as need and why a victim tries to change the situation by self-change in an effort to help the batterer and diffuse situation. In a relationship of abuse and violence these polarities become more and more rigid, each party is objectified, and in the lack of mutual recognition, subjectivity, and life itself, is diminished, and perhaps ultimately destroyed. Partners caught in this rigid reiteration of an intersubjective/intrapsychic life diminishing form of relatedness are playing out a dynamic that forms all of us to some extent, yet is individualized by particular convergences of a multitude of individual/cultural identifications[54] and historical factors.

But how does the power of interrelatedness working in culture work both to regulate and create subjects and subjectivity? Once again this power is ambiguous, like the power of God as that which is the power before good and evil, or the power of object relations which work both for enriched and diminished relationships, it moves both ways at once and turns on itself over and over again. Butler, like Benjamin, is concerned with the question of the subordinate's seeming attachment to subordination. When the subordinate seems to pursue her own subordination, not unlike what is done when battered women return to batterers or fail to press charges, then she could be held responsible for her own oppression. But Butler maintains that "the attachment to subjection is produced through the workings of power, and that part of

53. Miller, *Psychology of Women*; Miller and Stiver, *Healing Connection*.
54. Benjamin, *Like Subjects, Love Objects*, 49–79, suggests that we remember that gender identify is but one identification persons make and that gender identity itself is more complex than simply male or female. Thus intimate partner violence is not solely about gender, as apparent in same sex relationships, but about a multitude of factors.

the operation of power is made clear in this psychic effect, one of the most insidious of its productions."[55] In fact there is no subject without a "passionate attachment"[56] to those who do the subordinating because without them one would not be a subject at all.

The power of culture is usually thought of as a power that acts upon us for restriction and regulation, as if the power of culture were separate from the power that brings us into "being," as if power were itself a "metaphysical subject," as Butler describes it.[57] But if, as I have argued, all power is derived from the power of dynamic interrelatedness then the power of culture must also be such a derivative. The power of culture to which we are subjected, that we are thereby acted upon, is rooted in our desire to be, to live, to exist, which requires relationship. To be a person means to be recognized as such by others, which means to be subject to others but also to be a subject, to recognize others. Power at work in psychical development or in cultural subjection turns or "recoils"[58] on itself, acting on and in and through. In Butler's words, "The one who holds out the promise of continued existence plays to the desire to survive. 'I would rather exist in subordination than not exist' is one formulation of this predicament (where the risk of 'death' is also possible)."[59] Not unlike Fairbairn, Butler points out that the abuse of children is an exploitation of the desire to love and be loved when loving and being loved is the very stuff of existence. There is no possibility of a choice not to form attachments, especially in the state of dependency in early childhood or, I might add in abusive adult relationships, if attachment is required for life itself. Thus once again we return to a core ambivalence in human personhood born out of the ambiguous nature of the power of life.

According to Butler, and congruent with the theory of psyche posed here, subject formation requires an identification with the norms of culture, a prior subjection to the rules of culture. Identification, in object relations terms, means the introjection of a relationship such that in the introjection itself the ego/subject comes into being. I have

55. Butler, *Psychic Life of Power*, 6.
56. Ibid., 7.
57. Butler, *Bodies That Matter*, 9.
58. Butler, *Psychic Life of Power*, 96.
59. Ibid., 7.

argued that in the introjection the norms of culture that shape relationship become who we are. It is not that there are persons who, as pre-introjection persons, will then introject but rather that in the introjection which enables us to be persons the norms of culture are what constitutes that introjection. Thus, as Butler argues, a subject comes to be through a process of subjection to norms that requires an assumption of those norms. The citational power of the norms comes through a prior identification which means that we are the norms we cite.[60] In the "turning of power," at the very moment of the turn, when the other is internalized as object and a new subject is becoming, culture is not outside us (as if there was an "us" before the turn when in fact there is not) the culture is us. If cultural prescriptions such as the assumption of an appropriate amount of violence in families, the objectification of women, and other patriarchal ideologies contribute to intimate partner violence and it is in and of this kind of culture that persons develop and are made, then we need to look at how these cultural dynamics work to bring about not only the cooperation of participants but also creation of the participants.

Summary

This chapter has put forth a theory of psyche as constructed in and of culture. The one life instinct (libido), the energy of becoming through interrelatedness, manifests itself in the psyche as internal object relations that are representations of relationships with others from whom we are distinct but not separate. Persons develop in and through the need to love and be loved because of primordial interrelationship. The psyche matures through qualities of relatedness born out of the historical interactions between persons and their internal object relations, both conscious and unconscious. In the face of relationships upon which we depend for our very life and yet are always to various extents both fulfilling and unfulfilling, relationships are internalized as a means of protection from the possibility of losing relationship all together, which would be death itself. This identification of self with the other, internalized as object relations, offers the possibility of controlling and thus holding on to relationship, when any relationship, good or bad, is better than none. Under the pressure of the ambivalence that is then at

---

60. Butler, *Bodies That Matter*, and *Psychic Life of Power*.

the core of our psyche, some pieces of the object relations are split off from our consciousness and repressed in the unconscious, but nevertheless significantly influence behavior. Thus relationships with others may be marked by fluid and multiple or rigid and limited patterns of interaction.

It is clear then that the psyche comes into being in the process of internalization such that at its core the person is made of relationship. Development of the psyche happens over time, out of a history of interactions with the world. These interactions are between two subjects, and in these two present subjects convergence of all dynamic interrelatedness through time, which explains why they are always experienced with ambivalence. These two subjects are dependent upon one another; change in the interaction; continually internalize, split, repress, integrate and reintegrate; and become someone new and different in every moment. Mutual recognition of subjectivity, which involves recognition of an ontological difference, dependence and relatedness, is essential to becoming a subject and thus a person. To love and be loved, to give and receive, is essential for personhood. When rigidity and polarization of these two modes of relating, giving and receiving, as in intimate partner violence, the personhood of both parties is diminished and the whole web of life is damaged.

The activity, what is done, including the ascription of meaning, in relationship is the stuff of the psyche. Interaction in relationship requires a certain "shared reality" determined by culture which preexists the birth of any subject. Culture is this activity of meaning making between subjects which then also determines the content and form of the relationships of which the psyche is constructed. The workings of power in culture then assure that this "reality" persists through the creation of subjects who must adhere to cultural prescriptions in order to exist at all. No person comes into being without first being recognized as a subject based on the cultural laws for subjectivity. No subject position is made available or assigned to any thing/being unless certain prescriptions for what counts as subjectivity are met. There are no subjects who take on these prescriptions; the prescriptions pre-exist the subject and the prescriptions performatively bring the subject into being. There is then a core ambivalence to the psyche and personhood born out of the ambiguity inherent in power that is required for personhood and subjects those persons to multiple hegemonies, including gender, that are both life-giving and life-diminishing. The conscious and unconscious are thus formed by and made of culture as it forms and makes relationships such that there is nothing of the psyche that lies before or outside of culture.

But what of agency and the capacity to act in resistance to the culture of which the psyche is made? Such an exposition of the construction and constitution of the psyche will require a theory of agency that arises not from a pre-cultural core self or true self but from the nature of power working in culture and the process of construction itself. Since there is no self outside of or before culture, an understanding of the agency behind resistance will require a configuration of culture, in a sense, resisting itself. Chapter 5 will take up these matters of agency but prior to that another question must be attended to. What has happened to the body? At the outset of this book it was made clear that any theory/theology of human personhood based in the context of intimate partner violence must take into account the material or body in relation to the psyche. What is the relationship between the body and psyche and how do we understand those as mutually constituted of culture? These questions are taken up in the next chapter.

4

The Constructed Body

It is crucial to the thesis of this book that body and mind are seen as equally significant and mutually constitutive. I am proposing that persons can be identified as deeply constructed in and constituted of culture as inseparably psyche and body, and that agency arises precisely in and from that construction. Cultural construction cannot exclude the body or split the body from the psyche if the sensibilities of feminist theory and pastoral theology, as well as the care for victims of intimate partner violence, are respected. In the dynamics of intimate partner violence bodies are at stake, the physical survival of the participants is often the bottom line in these relationships. We are not only talking about emotional attachments but of bodily needs—food, shelter, work, and bodily integrity. Lived out on multiple planes, violent relationships teach us much about the inextricability of those planes. The batterer's use of power for control moves coextensively through control of body and psyche as constructed by and of a culture that likewise controls the body/psyches of women. The body and psyche are of the same time and space; thus to control one is to control the other. Verbal, physical, and cultural assaults are deeply intertwined such that any assaultive act results in harm to all. We recall that physical violence is usually preceded by verbal violence. I suggest that this is not a matter of degree, as in from the lesser of verbal abuse proceeding to the more serious physical abuse, or coincidence, but rather an indication of how well we know, if only intuitively, that language, psyche, and body are radically related. To be a person is to be made of body, psyche, and culture, not as three related but distinct substances, but as coextensive aspects of human personhood. The statement of the most severely traumatized,

"I am not a person," seems evidence of this interrelatedness.[1] To be a person requires psyche, body, and cultural recognition as such.

Chapter three explored the specifics in the construction of the psyche to illuminate the psychocultural dynamics at work in intimate partner violence. However the context of intimate partner violence and the current evolutions of feminist theory and pastoral theology insist that our thinking cannot stop there. That which might have been at one time understood as primarily individual psychopathology must now be placed in the context of embodied material life in a web of sociocultural relations. These sociocultural arrangements are lived out in and through bodies with material needs and practices. The "pathology" of the individual mind cannot be separated from the "pathology" of the culture nor can it be understood apart from the body in and through which the "pathology" is inflicted and experienced. The previous chapter suggested that there is nothing of the psyche that stands outside of or before culture, thus, in order to keep the commitments named above, the same must be said of the body and not only in relation of body to culture but of body to psyche. The three, while different, are not extricable, nor understandable, apart from one another.

Feminist theory has warned, however, that to speak of the cultural construction of body can easily be a means by which the limitations and oppressions of the body are obscured. Additionally, since the split of mind/body into a dualism has been by feminists attributed to patriarchal ideology, a feminist theory of the cultural construction of body must not perpetuate a split that opposes nature to culture. The power of interrelatedness cannot be solely affective, mental, or symbolic. The commitments established at the outset of this project require a theory of body that erases neither the limited and constrained nor the agential character of the body.

This chapter will explore how psyche and culture work in, with and through body, how they make each other. First, a look at the relation of psyche and body as understood through the object relations presented in chapter three, which already identified psyche as constituted of culture, will set the ground for understanding the body as also constituted of and constructed by culture. Butler, augmented by others such as Susan Bordo and Pierre Bourdieu, then offers a view and analysis of the

---

1. Herman, *Trauma and Recovery*, 94; see chapter 3 above.

body that calls into question the distinctions commonly made between nature and culture as those distinctions relate to embodied persons. Following this discussion of how it is that the body is constructed of culture, Paula Cooey's work lends a closer consideration of the deep interconnection in mind, body, and culture as evidenced by bodies in pain. Finally, this chapter, with the one preceding, will prepare the theoretical grounding for understanding agency, to be developed in chapter five, as emerging out of this coextensive construction of body/psyche where body does not get relegated to a secondary source of agency.

Body and Object Relations

For Fairbairn the body is not the source of libido but libido is that which energizes the body in relationships. The body is not the source of libidinal (relational) energy, nor is bodily pleasure or satisfaction the aim of libido, it is the means by which relatedness happens. Relationship is experienced through body. Speaking and listening, feeding and being fed, holding and being held are embodied acts. Fairbairn calls the body the "path of least resistance" for libidinal energy; it is the most immediate and easiest way for connection to another.[2] Fairbairn suggests that bodily pleasure is essentially about relationship, beginning in early development through basic bodily functions and through multiple channels with the increasing complexity of maturity. "In infancy, owing to the constitution of the human organism, the path of least resistance to the object happens to lie almost exclusively through the mouth; and the mouth accordingly becomes the dominant libidinal organ."[3] The mouth, through for instance, sucking, eating, and crying, is the primary means through which infants experience dependency and connection to others. This does not negate biological needs, i.e. for food, but insists that dynamic interrelatedness, or growth through interrelatedness, is the means by which biological needs are satisfied and given meaning.

Likewise the body emerges and derives from the web of relations. The body does not appear intact and fully developed. The dynamic energy, becomingness, the movement toward more, which operates through interrelationship, brings the body, its processes and organs and senses, into being. That beingness of the body is complex, multidi-

2. Fairbairn, *Psychoanalytic Studies*, 31.
3. Ibid., 32.

mensional and dynamic, as is the relational web itself, made of energy, not substance. The biological is not separate from the relational but is created out of the relational and the relational is generated out of the biological. The two "constitute perpetual cycles of mutual influence," as Mitchell states it.[4] The body develops; it does not arrive on the scene intact and finished but rather evolves in interaction with all the temporal and spatial influences of the web. The body is shaped and given meaning in interaction; the innate is not fixed or determinative but responds and grows in the context of the relational web that gives it life.

The relational context of the web shapes and creates the body but the body also shapes and creates relationship. They come into being together. In terms of the mind/body relationship, the body in its function, morphology, behavior, and all its activities from the beginning develops *with* the psyche. Although Fairbairn does not elaborate on this point in terms of the nature of bodily development, it does seem that, with the expansion of his theory that I have proposed, the body and body experienced can be understood as coming into being coextensively. There is no body without psyche and no psyche without body, as one develops so does the other. If one is damaged the other is damaged. This relationship of psyche/body is not that they exist side by side and grow parallel but that they are indeed not separate or distinguishable. We cannot tell where the psyche stops and the body begins or vice versa. It is through the satisfaction and frustration of relational needs that both the psyche and the body grow and the movements of one come in and through the movements of the other. The need for relatedness expressed in the hunger of a dependent infant requires two beings, someone to feed her or him and the infant to take in the food. The satisfaction or frustration holds both affective and physical significance. Internal object relations that are the content and structure of the psyche are born out of and made by these biologically based, bodily practiced, and sensory experienced interactions. Jane Flax reminds us that researchers of the brain are continually confronted with the "ghost in the machine problem," the fact that the brain has subjective qualities and cannot be understood solely in physiological or neurological terms.[5] Neither can the psyche be

---

4. Mitchell, *Relational Concepts*, 4.
5. Flax, *Disputed Subjects*, 98.

understood apart from the brain nor other bodily realities that provide the material for the internalized relations that are the psyche.

As stated in chapter three, the person develops intersubjectively, a dynamic of mutual recognition of subjectivity, and the moment of recognition of the other as subject is also the moment of internalization. The psyche is then constructed of these internalizations but this recognition of the other as subject occurs primarily through the body's needs and sensations. The most obvious boundary between persons is that of skin, morphology itself, but that morphology is not fixed, it is constantly changing and being shaped, developing because of and with the psyche and relationship. The practices that accompany the feeding of the infant require mutual recognition of body as subject that occurs only in the instant of internalization. As the body grows in complexity so does the psyche and the assignation to a subject position requires a body/psyche. There are no subjects, and therefore no persons, who are not body/psyche; no disembodied subjects, no disembodied psyches, and no living human bodies that are not also psyche.

The psyche is constructed in and constituted of culture; the internal object relations that make and make up the psyche are made of and by culture. If the psyche is made in and of culture, and the body and psyche are made of and make each other, then it is logically argued that the body is constructed likewise. The infant is born into a field of practices that have a long history and which any newborn, at least any newborn given a subject position, will immediately begin to internalize as self. Relationships are established and maintained because of a shared reality that must include, of course, shared practices in everything from language to how to hold one's body when walking. Excavations of the history of practices, in childrearing for instance, reveal the depth to which we have conflated historical construction with what is "naturally" embodied. Appeals to biology, when examined closely enough, reveal biological subjection to the psychical and cultural over time. Embodied practices are not subject to the motivation of the psyche but form the body and the psyche that in turn form the practices out of the motivation for life in the web of interrelatedness that is body/psyche/culture. Practices and meanings preexist the body/psyche in the cultural milieu of the web. Neither the biological material nor the development of that material exists prior to or untouched by culture. The body, coextensively with the psyche, is made of and by culture.

Construction of the Body

To argue that the body is, along with the psyche, constructed of and by culture is, as I stated previously, not to argue that the body is not "real" or that it does not represent limitations and determinations for what it means to be person. It does mean that concessions to what is irreducible about the body must be questioned for their political meanings. A constructed body also demands that we question references to the body as they set the boundary lines between body and mind and between psyche, person, and culture. Butler suggests that it is in the concession to anatomy, physiology, biology, etc. that the body is materialized. The concession *is* the drawing of the line, a selecting of what counts as material, or innate (when understood as a pre-cultural fixed aspect of personhood), and what does not. The body could be seen as a surface upon which the psyche and culture act which would suggest that there is a pre-social body. But how is a pre-social body produced in an ontologically interrelated world? The body could be that which exceeds psyche and culture, that which holds out a portion at least of person that is untarnished by oppressive regimes of culture which have taken hold of our minds and souls. But where is this untarnished place? Is not the designation of the tarnished and untarnished also subject to the language and practices of the hegemony?

Body and Language

Any positing of a body as ontologically separate from culture and psyche refers to an ontological dualism between psyche and body, a problem addressed previously in chapter two. Butler suggests that we think of matter as "a process of materialization that stabilizes over time to produce the effect of boundary, fixity, and surface we call matter."[6] Once again we are reminded to think in terms of energy and activity rather than substance.

> It must be possible to concede and affirm an array of "materialities" that pertain to the body, that which is signified by the domains of biology, anatomy, physiology, hormonal and chemical composition, illness, age, weight, metabolism, life and death. None of this can be denied. But the undeniability of these "materialities" in no way implies what it means to affirm them, in-

---

6. Butler, *Bodies That Matter*, 9.

deed, what interpretive matrices condition, enable and limit that necessary affirmation. That each of those categories have a history and a historicity, that each of them is constituted through the boundary lines that distinguish them and, hence, by what they exclude, that relations of discourse and power produce hierarchies and overlappings among them and challenge those boundaries, implies that these are *both* persistent and contested regions.[7]

It is important to understand that this questioning of the construction of bodies is not to say that bodies do not matter, but rather to insist actually that bodies do indeed matter significantly and therefore require examination and "unsettling," as Butler says, in order to find "new ways for bodies to matter."[8] In the radical interrelatedness proposed here neither psyche nor body exceeds the other. The line between that which is named body and that which is named psyche has shifted and changed through time. Butler suggests that it is in the drawing of the line that the split between the interior and the exterior is fabricated and that the body materializes. The fact that the line is *drawn* rather than ontologically given suggests that it is produced by cultural prescriptions which serve a political purpose. If we are interested in resistance and change, then we must question the drawing and the material that is conceded as "natural" as the result of the line.

Butler suggests that it is the need for language that inextricably binds psyche and body. The persistence of materiality, according to Butler,

> [I]s a *demand in and for language*, a "that which" which prompts and occasions, say, within the domain of science, calls to be explained, described, diagnosed, altered or within the cultural fabric of lived experience, fed, exercised, mobilized, put to sleep, a site of enactments and passions of various kinds. To insist upon this demand, this site, as the "that without which" no psychic operation can proceed, but also as that on which and through which the psyche also operates, is to begin to circumscribe that which is invariably and persistently the psyche's site of operation; not the blank slate or passive medium upon which the psyche acts, but, rather, the constitutive demand that mobilizes psychic action from the start, that is that very mobilization,

---

7. Ibid., 66–67.
8. Ibid., 30.

and, in its transmuted and projected bodily form, remains that psyche.[9]

It is then the need for that shared reality necessitated by the ontological reality of intersubjectivity that binds psyche and body in their co-emergence. The language and practices of culture give form and shape to body and psyche, not so that either is reduced to culture, or that they are only culture. We cannot collapse body, psyche, and culture into each other. They are different, yet never totally, and never separate.

In *Gender Trouble* Butler argues that we must rethink theories of gender that propose gender as the social construction of sex norms imposed upon a body naturally sexed at birth. Although this book is not focused on the construction of sex/gender, Butler's thought on the subject illustrates the way the body (sex) is constructed and constituted of culture (gender).

> Gender ought not to be conceived merely as the cultural inscription of meaning on a pre-given sex (a juridical conception); gender must also designate the very apparatus of production whereby the sexes themselves are established. As a result, gender is not to culture as sex is to nature; gender is also the discursive/cultural means by which "sexed nature" or a "natural sex" is produced and established as "prediscursive," prior to culture, a politically neutral surface *on which* culture acts.[10]

Prior to the birth of a sexed body is a gender system that normalizes two sexes, male and female, and then categorizes every body into one or the other. This system of classification over time takes on the appearance of a "natural" occurrence—two kinds of bodies, male and female—and makes it a condition of subjectivity.[11] Woman (or girl or female) should be seen as a performative identity, a speech act that constitutes identity, not a representational identity, or an identity that simply refers to what is given or obvious. Gender is not a social construction that is imposed upon a pre-social body that is naturally sexed, or that is anchored in the psyche as a result of pre-social sexually driven bodies, but is the social

---

9. Ibid., 67.

10. Butler, *Gender Trouble*, 7.

11. Butler argues that this genderization of sex sustains the hegemonic regime of heterosexuality. I do not here engage that argument but use her point as an illustration of the social construction of the body.

repetition of norms that constitutes sexed bodies. "[T]he construction 'compels' our belief in its necessity and naturalness."[12]

Once again, as Mitchell encouraged us to do with object relations, we must move from spatial metaphors to temporality. The "appearance of substance" happens over time, rather than as a fixture in space, in a "stylized repetition of acts through time," what Butler also calls the "corporealization of time."[13] This construction is exposed precisely in its limitations and in the necessity for repetition as bodies also continuously fail to fit or comply with the rules of gender/sex. As we will see in the next chapter it is the possibility of this failure that is also the site of agency and the possibility of resistance. The culture of gender distinction both regulates identities/bodies and is at the same time a precondition for subjectivity itself. There are, after all, no unsexed/ungendered persons. To argue that sex is a construction of gender does not negate the realities of gender or sex identity as they are construed in a culture of gender hegemony. The construction of a body as female or as woman is certainly not insignificant when her body is beaten precisely because her body is a "woman's" body. But of course culture is also created, reiterated and yet constantly revised. It is here in this dynamic of construction, this movement of revision and reiteration between culture, body, and psyche that we will find agency and the possibility of resistance.

The Body Practiced

In Butler's schema a person emerges in a position of intelligibility made possible by speech in the matrices of culture, including conventional practices. This section will elaborate on the practical body, the body that moves, operates, and feels as a carrier and reiteration of culture. Social identity is constituted in and of everyday practices, modes of standing, walking, eating, for instance, all of which appear to be "naturally" unconstructed but are in fact the practices of certain social structures. As a way of accompanying Butler, I turn first to the practice theory of Pierre Bourdieu and then to the work on the particular practical regulation of women's bodies, as expounded on by feminist Susan Bordo.

Bourdieu suggests that there is a "practical sense" embedded in the bodied subject and in social fields. This practical sense is a certain "logic

12. Butler, *Gender Trouble*, 140.
13. Ibid., 1–41.

of practice" that is not the logic of reason, not rational but nonetheless reasonable and systematic.[14] Practice follows rules and models up to a point; at that point the logic of reason fails and the logic of practice sets in. In the face of a failure to account for activity as reasoned and organized intention, Bourdieu suggests the "ordering principle" for bodily activity can be found in the "incorporated dispositions, or more precisely the body schema," which is "capable of orienting practices in a way that is at once unconscious and systematic."[15] The ordering principle is not logic or reason but practice itself and the "practical sense" that makes it possible for us to act in a way that "makes sense." The appearance of coherence, of a smooth flow of action—reaction, of repetitive sequences, proceeds from a historically reactivated schema of bodily movement. The body "functions as a practical operator" following a practical logic where the right hand reaches to the left to meet a hand extended from another's right.[16] This practical sense is "what makes it possible to appreciate the meaning of the situation instantly, at a glance, in the heat of the action, and to produce at once the opportune response."[17] It is a state of the body, a "belief" that is matter itself.

Bourdieu calls these structuring dispositions of the body, "habitus." Habitus is the social in the body, directing and producing the "right" act at the "right" time and in the "right" place. But habitus is not only activity; it is the socially constructed "categories of perception and assessment" and "classificatory principles"[18] deeply rooted in and necessary for the recognition of the subject. Through habitus social structures, institutions, language, and discourse are incorporated into "spontaneous" bodily responses making the simplest of actions appear apolitical, a necessity, when in fact they are historically conditioned. "[T]he whole social order imposes itself at the deepest level of the bodily dispositions through a particular way of regulating the use of time, the temporal distribution of collective and individual activities and the appropriate rhythm with which to perform them."[19] These internalized bodily

---

14. Bourdieu, *Logic of Practice*.
15. Ibid., 10.
16. Ibid., 93.
17. Ibid., 104.
18. Bourdieu, *In Other Words*, 13.
19. Bourdieu, *Logic of Practice*, 75.

dispositions ensure the hegemonic "correctness" of practice by their reactivation over time of schemas of perception and appreciation that endure in matter thereby assuring that, to use Butler's terms, what "matters" endures.

These regularities of practice exist beyond consciousness, introspection or will, beyond the "rules" or explicitly stated principles. The "rules" cannot communicate the "feel for the game" which comes only through practice and is not divisible into units of movement or describable in words. "Practical sense, social necessity turned into nature, converted into motor schemes and body automatism, is what causes practices, in and through what makes them obscure to the eyes of their producers, to be *sensible*, that is, informed by common sense."[20] "Common sense" is produced in and through the structural mechanisms of society, "generating practices that are convergent and objectively orchestrated outside of a collective 'intention' or consciousness, let alone 'conspiracy.'"[21] This is a temporal process, acquired in time and development but not conscious or intentional, rather a necessity for that which counts as personhood and life itself. Habitus functions as the past presently anticipating the future without conscious direction. Given the action and reaction of the past, the future appears immanent, a constructed necessity unknown as such. A step, a turn, or a reach anticipate, without awareness, another step, turn, and reach and yet at the same time the assumption about the "next step" brings the probable into being, appearing then to be a given, and obscuring the possibility of questioning the necessity of the action. The "feel for the game" gives one a sense of what will happen next and then un(or sub)consciously makes it happen.

Bordo's work elaborates on the many practices that culture uses to regulate, determine, and objectify, and thus deny subjectivity to women.[22] First, Bordo argues, as do many feminist theorists,[23] that woman's body cannot be understood apart from the dualism that has not only

---

20. Ibid., 69.
21. Bourdieu and Wacquant, *Reflexive Sociology*, 124.
22. Bordo, *Unbearable Weight*. Bordo critiques Butler for an overemphasis on language suggesting that Butler, in Gender Trouble, loses the regulated and determining aspect of culture. I disagree with Bordo's assessment, and think that in her later work Butler clarifies some of the points with which Bordo takes issue, but it is not necessary to engage that debate here in order to develop the point I am making here.
23. For instance, see the essays in Jaggar and Bordo, *Gender/Body/Knowledge*.

split mind and body and devalued body but has gendered that split by equating woman with body; thus devaluing women. Historically in Western thought the body has been understood as that which is a limitation to the more desirable—pure reason, true self. The body is known as "animal, as appetite, as deceiver, as prison of the soul, and confounder of its projects,"[24] something that must be overcome, resisted, and transcended. Even the current climate of "obsession" with the body is not about accepting body but controlling it by the power of our will. If woman is understood to represent body then woman is also animal, confounder and something to be overcome and disciplined. Woman as "temptress," seen as such simply because she is woman, brings out the "uncontrollable," the irrational in men who then blame the woman for their embodied practices in reaction. For instance, as Bordo describes it, "chronic wife-batterers often claim that their wives 'made them' beat them up, by looking at them the wrong way, by projecting too much cheek, or by some other (often very minor) bodily gesture of autonomy."[25] Women "ask for it" by virtue of their bodied presence as woman.

Bordo insists that the body is under the "grip" of culture through "the practices and bodily habits of everyday life."[26] The body is not just represented in culture, not a tabula rasa inscribed with meaning, but is a "living cultural form."[27] Everything from how we walk, sit, or stand, to our common gestures, to our eating and bathroom habits, not to mention the many ways we adorn bodies, are derived from culture and then make and shape our bodies. None of the material of the body in all of its practices and in the most unconscious of bodily processes, like breathing or the pulsing of our blood, escapes culture. For instance what one eats or does not eat may be seen as a matter of personal choice but in actuality is a matter of the personal intersecting with the cultural where the culture determines the range of appropriate "foods," strongly influenced by capitalism which creates desires, making them become needs, and then those "foods" also shape our morphology and will directly affect the makeup of our bodily fluids. Over time human bodies change in order to adapt to culture. This should not be construed to mean that

24. Bordo, *Unbearable Weight*, 3.
25. Ibid., 7.
26. Ibid., 16.
27. Ibid., 287.

there ever exists an uncultured body that then becomes altered under the pressures of culture. Culture pre-exists the body.

Body is a "medium of culture," a "metaphor for culture," a "text of culture," and a "practical, direct locus of social control."[28] Under gender hegemony women's bodies are, as are men's, regulated and made to serve the ruling ideology. Once again power used unilaterally is life diminishing, subjectivity denying, and is, when used more mutually and reciprocally, life enriching. Women's bodies under patriarchal control are made for the pleasure of the other, the one in control. One way culture works is to conform a person's desires and beliefs to the dominant. Another way that culture works is to conform a person's body. Bordo describes the insidiousness of this practical and material control:

> Not chiefly through ideology, but through the organization and regulation of the time, space, and movements of our daily lives, our bodies are trained, shaped, and impressed with the stamp of prevailing historical forms of selfhood, desire, masculinity, femininity. Such an emphasis casts a dark and disquieting shadow across the contemporary scene. For women, as study after study shows, are spending more time on the management and discipline of our bodies than we have in a long, long time. In a decade marked by a reopening of the public arena to women, the intensification of such regimens appears diversionary and subverting. Through the pursuit of an ever-changing, homogenizing, elusive ideal of femininity—a pursuit without a terminus, requiring that women constantly attend to minute and often whimsical changes in fashion-female bodies become docile bodies—bodies whose forces and energies are habituated to external regulation, subjection, transformation, "improvement." Through the exacting and normalizing disciplines of diet, makeup, and dress—central organizing principles of time and space in the day of many women—we are rendered less socially oriented and more centripetally focus on self-modification. Through these disciplines, we continue to memorize on our bodies the feel and conviction of lack, of insufficiency, of never being good enough. At the farthest extremes, the practices of femininity may lead us to utter demoralization, debilitation, and death.[29]

---

28. Ibid., 165.
29. Ibid., 166.

These "normal and everyday" dynamics are played out to their logical extreme on the bodies of battered women. Control is exercised through language, social discourse, and through the material practices of embodied subjects in which one body may use physical violence or the ever present "regulatory gaze"[30] to master the body of the other.

Bodies are made of and regulated by culture. In order to count as a subject one must walk like a subject and talk like a subject. These regulatory practices are not something that a person can consciously or intentionally opt out of. We participate because to not participate is to not exist. Bodies cannot be changed at will nor does our will escape regulation. As Bordo reminds us, "one is always somewhere."[31] Our bodies are located and limited. Any choice that is presented for bodily appearance or practice or transformation is a regulated choice, not only in terms of the range of choice but of the ideal of choice. When a victim of intimate partner violence remains in the home after a brutal beating it may appear to be by choice but the body, and in this case the regulated and beaten body, is not separate from imagination or will so that a controlled will is a controlled body and a controlled body is a controlled will.

The Experiencing and Experienced Body

The second area accompanying Butler's schema of body revolves around the body as that which forces the attribution or denial of subjectivity, and as an experiencing body that is dynamic and ambiguous. Paula Cooey, *Religious Imagination and the Body*, proposes that the body is both "artifact of culture" and "imagining subject."[32] Cooey is interested in looking at the body as a source of epistemological authority, particularly in terms of religious experience. She questions the relationship of body to culture and whether or not, and if so how, the body is a site for agency. The relation of "thought" and the "material" must be conceived

---

30. This is a phrase made known by the work of Michel Foucault and appropriated by Bordo, *Unbearable Weight*, 27, 273–75, to understand women's "self- correcting" gaze in the service of the rule of patriarchy.

31. Ibid., 229.

32. Cooey, *Religious Imagination*.

in ways that "prevent degeneration into biologism, on the one hand, and a lapse into ahistorical idealism, on the other hand."[33]

Cooey proposes that body be understood as both site and sign, as an ambiguously dynamic product of culture and as a creative agent of culture and resistance. As sign, the body forces the attribution or denial of subjectivity and thus "serves as a building block in the social construction of subjectivity, an attribution often denied particularly on grounds of racial, ethnic, class, and gender differences."[34] The very presence of a body "demands language" as Butler said, and yet also pushes the limits of language. Bodily presence requires a decision, either this body will count or be recognized as a subject, as one who knows, speaks, and influences or it will not. As I have stated before, everyone who is afforded the identity "person" is a subject to some extent but the degree of subjectivity is a cultural political ascription.[35] The subject, and therefore human personhood, is a product of a history of a cultural matrix of relations that remains for the most part unacknowledged and unknown. As Butler has also stated, the subject is constructed in and of these relations, and the body is a sign of this construction as it forces language, demands response, and is represented and imagined by culture. The gendered body of woman is a result of this historical chain of thought and action that can be known precisely by the presence of a "woman" gendered body. Of course, with recollection of the discussion on intersubjectivty in chapter three, if the body is a sign of subjectivity it is also a sign of being an object since every subject, in order to be a subject, is also the "other" or object of another subject. But Cooey makes the point that the extent to which subjectivity is attributed is an act of power "made in part by inference from the body."[36] The inferences made by the presence of certain bodies or bodily characteristics are both the product of past inferences and the basis for future inferences. The terms of the inferences are set but the body demands that they be made.

Body is also site, the place in which and through which imagination and creativity take place. Imagination is an intentional mental

---

33. Ibid., 71.

34. Ibid., 90.

35. Cooey, *Religious Imagination*, 47. I use the terms "subject" and "subjectivity" in a slightly different way than Cooey in the sense that I speak of the assignation of subject status and subjectivity in matters of degree rather than something one is or is not.

36. Ibid., 118.

process by which images of external objects are present in the mind but not to the physical senses. "Because the activity of imagining and the objects imagined depend on pre-existing social and material conditions, and because the objects are further shareable with others through visual, verbal, and audial symbol systems, imagination, both as activity and as condition, is necessarily social, however, individually exercised."[37] Imagination is required for agency as one must be able to imagine oneself acting if one is to act, bodily action and mental representation are linked although may not be consciously experienced in any particular chronological order. An action may be made without that action first consciously imagined, but once the act has occurred, it will be imagined, and it then demands to be taken into account. The sense experience must in every moment affect mental dynamics. As site of these dynamics and processes, according to Cooey, "the body as site serves both as a means for substantiating reality and, through sensation, as a driving force for projecting or imagining it; the body as sign serves as vocabulary in establishing and evaluating agency and relations of power and powerlessness by eliciting or cuing responses of attribution and denial."[38]

How exactly does sentience relate to culture? How can emotion, perception, and sensation, seemingly tied to bodily responses "out of our control" and due to "natural" physiological reaction, be understood as culturally constituted? As Cooey suggests these empirical events are the means by which reality is established, validated, and understood. This does not mean that sentience has any pre- or acultural truth. "Feelings do not provide access to reality beyond what culture validates as real."[39] Cooey draws upon work done in cognitive psychology[40] to explore "emotion in relation to sensation and language,"[41] suggesting that feeling is interpretive. Emotions are interpreted through culture, not "raw data more akin to sensation."[42] Emotion is accompanied by sensation but the meaning attributed to that emotion and the triggers

37. Ibid., 4–5.
38. Ibid., 119.
39. Ibid., 51.
40. Ibid., 46–51.
41. Ibid., 46.
42. Ibid., 47.

for those sensations are environmentally and culturally established. Certain kinds of situations elicit particular sensations, the sensations do not occur outside of or prior to a context. The sensations themselves are culture, an expression of meaning and power structures. Sensation never occurs as raw data. Feelings are an integration of body and language, where culture is bodily "experienced," iterated and reiterated.

The radical inseparability and coextensive nature of culture and body is particularly salient in bodies in pain. When a body is in extreme pain, as in extreme physical abuse, the connection between body, culture, and psyche breaks down. If they become completely separated then, given that the power of interrelatedness is the power of life itself, subjectivity ceases to exist, interrelationship is broken, and there is no person, no life. Cooey, looking at torture victims and drawing upon the work of Elaine Scarry,[43] unmasks the infliction of bodily injury and pain for the "fiction of power"[44] that it is.[45] I have proposed that the use of the power of interrelatedness for control of one by another may temporarily give the illusion of an increase in subjectivity for the perpetrator of violence, who may argue that the violence is out of love and concern for the relationship, but will ultimately decrease the subjectivity of all parties. The destruction carried out by torture accomplishes its aim in splitting imagination and pain. More pain means a reduction of imagination, the ability to hold internal mental objects, a sign of and necessity for subjectivity. In torture, as in intimate partner violence, the victim's own body is used as a "pedagogical tool" against the victim. The aim of this brutal pedagogy is not that which the perpetrator claims but is rather "the disembodiment of the torturer's identity and the destruction of the imagination, and thereby the identity and the world of the tortured."[46] In both the perpetrator and the victim, pain and imagination are split from one another, unable to be held together. For the victim with more violence comes more inability to imagine and speak, language breaks down, and bodily sensation reigns until there is nothing, no feeling, no language, and thus no subject, no person. The paradox for the victim is that even while the pain is an enemy, it is also a guarantee of existence.

43. Scarry, *Body in Pain*.

44. This term is used by Scarry and appropriated by Cooey in Cooey, "Re-Membering the Body," 30. Cooey uses it in reference to domestic violence.

45. Cooey, *Religious Imagination*, 57–61.

46. Cooey, "Re-Membering the Body."

The perpetrator must also split, for in order to inflict such pain one must not be able to imagine that pain in one's own body nor in the body of another.

Scarry suggests that it is in this destructive process that the creative process becomes evident, that the "unmaking" of the world reveals the "making of the world" in the body. As long as there is any connection between imagination and pain then there is subjectivity and as long as there is subjectivity there is life. Furthermore, if there is imagination and pain, then the making and unmaking, destruction and creativity, are both continuing since one requires the other. Making and unmaking do not happen outside of culture but are indeed signs of the cultural construction, which requires continual reiteration because the power of the construction is ambiguous and dynamic, moving for more and less, toward and away, constructing and deconstructing. The body is both site for imagination and the object of imagination.

Cooey suggests that the relationship of the body as site and sign is one of "mapping."[47] In mapping the body negotiates the constant tension and movement between sentience and subjectivity. In explanation of her choice of terminology Cooey states:

> Mapping is visual and spatial, as well as temporal and verbal. It further preserves a tension between materiality and discourse that I find lacking in such concepts as "interpreting" and "expressing," though "mapping" includes connotations of both. Furthermore, the activity of mapping captures simultaneously a visual detachment necessary to an aerial view and a sense of being in the middle of things seeking to convey direction.
>
> Mapping is an act of symbolic construction, an act of imagination; nevertheless, real cartographers, however agential, are subject to material conditions that they cannot control.[48]

The "mapping" that happens in and on the body is that restlessness, that dynamic event that makes the body what it is. It is the cycle of reiteration that Butler refers to and the repetition of pattern that creates what appears as substance but is in actuality event. Mapping is what persons do and what is done to persons as we live in this web of interrelatedness.

Cooey highlights the ambiguity and dynamism at the core of what it means to be bodied persons. The tension between the body as site and

---

47. Ibid., 90.
48. Ibid., 91.

sign of culture is the battleground of multiple and competing interpretations and practices.

> At the most fundamental level of experience mapping designates what counts as pain as opposed to pleasure, what counts as tolerable bodily sensation as opposed to intolerable, and in some cases even what a society or culture is willing to acknowledge as sensation at all. Mapping further defines the borders that distinguish public from private, by plotting what counts as appropriate activity for public disclosure, (for example, eating with your mouth closed) and what is restricted to the private domain (usually acts of sexual intercourse and biological elimination). Mapping most especially codes difference signified as gender, class, race, ethnicity, religious creed, level of education, and politics. Thus, the body is mapped from the outside in, as well as the inside out, and mapping, even at this most micrological level, reflects power struggles that are characteristically ideological.[49]

In these dynamics of mapping boundaries, of constantly regulating what counts in one category or another, culture forms and constitutes persons as body/psyche. Once again it is in this very dynamic of construction and its ambiguous power that we find the site of both constraint and regulation and agency and resistance.

Summary

This book aims to present a theological anthropology that locates the human agency needed for resistance in the cultural construction and constitution of human personhood. Thus, a theology of agency rests upon a theory/theology of cultural construction/constitution which has been the purpose of the three preceding chapters. Chapter two posited an ontological dynamic interrelatedness as the theological basis for a radical cultural construction of human personhood. The following two chapters expounded on the specific processes by which this construction occurs so that persons are understood as psyche/body/culture.

The notion of cultural construction/constitution of persons requires an ontology of dynamic interrelatedness, expressed theologically as God. God as the "organic restlessness" of the web is the whole of life, the power of life itself operating in its continuing "becomingness"

---

49. Ibid., 92.

through the vast web of interrelatedness. God is not one aspect of the whole of actuality but all actuality, in all its complexity, fluidity, multiplicity, paradox, ambivalence, and ambiguity. All power is derived from this power though it is ambiguous and can be used for or experienced as good and evil, that which provokes or draws us into more life and an enriched web of relations or into less life and a diminished web of relations.

The energy of this web is patterned into structures that may appear substantive but are event. When the power of interrelatedness is used unilaterally for control of one by another life is diminished. Corporately this results in structures of oppression, individually in structures of abuse, both of which are inextricable from each other and both of which result in bondage and loss of life for all parties and necessarily then for the whole of the web. When the power of interrelatedness is used mutually and reciprocally for enriched relationship, life for all flourishes. The structure of culture and individual relationship reflect and create justice, love, liberation, and increased subjectivity for all.

Persons emerge in this field of relationship and interaction, as a result of the historical chain of events leading to a particular moment in time of subjective actuality. Persons too are event, a coming together of many minute experiences into something that appears to remain the same over time but in actuality is always moving toward something else. Persons too are, of course, rooted in and made of those ontological actualities of becomingness, a dynamic energy moving in history toward the future through an interrelatedness in which any one movement moves through the whole. There is then not such thing as an unrelated person or a person who chooses to be related. We "live in each other" across time and space. Thus the cultural and the personal, the material and the psychical are inseparable, created by and from one another.

The psyche develops in this same mode by internalizing aspects of relationship as object relations and then integrating, splitting and repressing. This activity happens out of the fundamental need for relationship based on the ontological reality of interrelatedness. Development occurs in and through qualities of relationship affected by the extent to which internal relations, functioning to hold on to relationships under the threat of death as loss of relationship, can manage fluidity to hold the tension and ambiguity necessarily present in the intersubjective emergence of personhood. Internal relations are formed because of the intersubjective nature of interrelatedness that necessitates that some aspects of relationship will be experienced as frustrating or failing. Thus results the emergent core ambivalence; we cannot live without relationship and yet we cannot live with it in its failings, so we hold on by means of internalizing. It is the fear of non-relatedness and thus of death that has victims and perpetrators of abuse and oppression caught in these life diminishing, for all, dynamics.

Relationships are lived out in practice and given meaning in a cultural milieu that precedes any individual. The granting of a subject position required for personhood requires certain recognition by and participation in this culture. Culture and its many matrices is needed in order to have relationship at all by providing a means of "shared reality." The when, where, how, and what of internalization and splitting are determined by and made of culture. At the same time these dynamics, by virtue of being constantly disrupted and in need of reiteration, reintegration, or re-repression, are the creation of culture and thus resistance to culture as it has been.

As psyche is constructed so is body. Relationship is known and experienced through body, especially in early infancy through bodily needs, functions, and sensations. Like psyche and culture, body is made of the dynamic energy of interrelatedness, an event developing out of the organic restlessness that is God. When considering body and psyche and culture one cannot tell where one stops and the other begins. The body materializes over time, constructed in and of discourse, practice and experience. The body demands language and the attribution or denial of subjectivity. In practice as subject it forces response or reaction and it is a means by which control is practiced.

Intimate partner violence has been linked to the assignation of women's bodies as "woman" in a culture that has not only equated women to body but has then devalued both. Bodies designated "woman" are representative of all that is body and in need of regulation, which of course serves to keep the ruling hegemony in tact. Beating then is understood as a logical extension of regulation that also includes more "acceptable" forms such as that of dress and appearance. In many respects intimate partner violence confirms Butler's premise that there are "bodies that matter" and are therefore subjects, and bodies that don't, what she calls "abjects."[50] The bodies of domestic violence victims have historically seemed to matter very little in a culture that has deemed them "appropriate" victims. There has been something the matter with the violent materialization of oppression in the private sphere, but historically domestic matters have not been appropriately taken up as public matters. Furthermore, historically the male head of the household, and most often the perpetrator of violence, was ascribed more subjectivity than the woman who under the violence was dematerializing or losing what subjectivity she might have had. Although, as I have stated previously, ultimately in the context of on-going escalating violence the subjectivity of all parties will "dematerialize."

Everything that is referred to as body is subject to culture. As Cooey points out, there is no such thing as the "raw" data of sensation and experience. It is always mediated through and constituted of culture. Bodies then are not to be trusted as a site of "pure" untarnished knowledge or agency and imagination. The body is ambiguous in that it is both creative and constrained, the site of both the making of culture in its regulations and abuse and in its unmaking, precisely because it is a dynamic event in which these processes are forever "battling" or shifting, forming and reforming the body. It is in fact, according to Cooey, the body in pain, as in intimate partner violence, that this "battle" and the ambiguity of regulation and agency is most evident. In this kind of extreme sensation, the body, psyche, culture are split and if allowed to follow its "natural" course will lead to the death of subjectivity and thus personhood. This process of destruction provides evidence of, and to some extent (not to death) is necessary for, the process of creation needed for agency.

The ground, however shifting and unsettlingly unstable, is thus set for thinking about the origins and sites of agency, as rooted in this radical cultural construction, and as shown to us through countless acts of resistance on the part of victims of intimate partner violence.

---

50. Butler, *Bodies That Matter*.

5

A Pastoral Theology of Human Agency

A CENTRAL PURPOSE OF THIS BOOK IS TO EXPLORE THE ORIGINS OF human agency as it is implicated in the actions of victims of intimate partner violence. Pastoral care providers are ultimately concerned with change and the amelioration of suffering, which requires agency. In this work of pastoral theology, victims, and the practices of care with them, are looked to as both a source of theological questions and as a source of theological knowledge, so that they are both recipients of application and agents of construction. We learn from the dynamics of intimate partner violence that care and change require resistance to oppression as it forms both persons and worlds. I am therefore suggesting that victims of intimate partner violence have much to teach us about agency, a prerequisite for resistance. Pastoral theologians are then necessarily concerned with the origins and workings of agency as necessary for care and for the promotion of increased, or more liberated, subjectivity.

A feminist view of intimate partner violence links the problem to women's oppression in a patriarchal society. Both feminism and the battered women's movement have based their political movements on a publicly identifying of women as victims of injustice, an injustice that sustains domestic violence. As victims of cultural and societal injustice they are in need of assistance, attention, and healing. However, as a movement, and as individuals who show great courage and strength in changing their own lives, they are also agents of personal and social change. It is important, then, that any theology of human agency keep the tension between persons as acted upon, or victims of culture, and as actors, or agents of culture. As stated earlier, too much agency negates the necessity for resistance and too little the possibility.

The previous chapters set forth a proposal for thinking of persons, mind and body, as constructed by and constituted of culture. However up until now we have primarily described culture as acting upon persons, or as determinative of persons. The culture of patriarchal oppression has formed the bodies and minds of persons so that they often live out this oppression in violent intimate relationships. It might seem that there is no escape, no possibility of liberation, that human actions are completely determined by the culture in which we live. But culture is clearly also an expression or creation of persons. We are both "constituted and constituting" subjects.[1] How is it that culture makes persons and persons make culture? What happens in the power of interrelatedness as it works in the cultural constructions of persons that enables things to change, to resist the continual reenactment or reiteration of oppression? How are we to understand the possibility that victims and perpetrators and those that care with and for them can resist that culture when they are made of it, when their feelings, thoughts, and behaviors are the expressions of cultural hegemonies?

Agency, broadly speaking, is the capacity to act. Human action is an expression of subjectivity, an extension of the subject into the world such that there is an event that has an effect external to and beyond the subject. The tension that arises in any discussion of agency is whether or not the act is self, or otherwise, determined. The debate arises over the extent to which our actions are under our own control. Do we determine and freely choose our actions or are they determined for us? Are we active participants in the world or "passive conduits" for social and psychological forces?[2] Absolute determinism means that whatever happens is caused by prior conditions and that any particular event is the *only* thing that could have happened given the conditions; that we had no alternative but to act the way we did. In contrast to absolute determinism is absolute free agency, in which there are infinite possibilities and alternatives from which we can choose without any restriction or limitations placed upon us from external sources. Susan Hekman describes the dichotomy this way: "the *constituting* subject is the subject of free will, the subject that determines his place in life, that forges his destiny, that decides to be free. The *constituted* subject, on

---

1. Hekman, "Subjects and Agents."
2. Meyers, "Agency."

the other hand, is determined, a product of social forces rather than their creator, a social dupe [italics mine]."³ The practical ramifications of these differing positions are crucial in the attribution of responsibility and the question of to what extent persons can be held accountable for their behavior and life situations. In the context of intimate partner violence the tension between these two perspectives arises, for example, in debates about criminal prosecution of perpetrators or what makes victims stay in violent relationships. To what extent can perpetrators be held accountable for their actions, given the culture in which they live, the external pressures to which they are subjected, and the psychological traumas from which they may suffer? To what extent should victims be recipients of public protection, assistance and sympathy given their personal choices, their rejection of the help offered, and their ability to competently function in many other areas of their lives?

There is an assumption in the dichotomy posed above that the internal or inner world of the person is free of the external. To speak of self-determined action is to state something of the motivation for and cause of action and to assume that, presuming a theory of an autonomous subject, the motivation can arise in an inner space that can operate outside of the pressures of external forces. However, this project has proposed that the internal and external cannot be separated, that there is no "self," or part of a self, free of external forces, therefore to speak of self-determined action at least must mean something different then might be supposed. But how is action determined? To what extent can persons "choose" their actions? Does the subject have a "will" and to what extent is it "free?" It is clear from the argument thus far that under the theory and theology I am proposing here, there is no possibility of unconstrained choice or action. Agency cannot arise from a place outside of external forces if both the internal and external are made of culture. It is, in fact, the thesis of this book that, following Judith Butler, agency *cannot* arise from a pre-cultural place and does arise from the very culture that one might use agency to resist. Agency, in fact, *necessitates* a theory/theology of cultural construction.

In general the question of agency from the perspective of personality theory revolves around issues related to motivation/desire, the existence of the conscious and unconscious, and the work of repression.

3. Hekman, "Subjects and Agents," 202.

To what extent do we will or desire our own misery and to what extent can we will ourselves out of it? Freud's major contribution to personality theory was the idea that by far the majority of our internal psychic activity is completely unknown to us, that our foremost and most basic reasons for acting the way we do and being the persons we are reside outside our awareness; and furthermore we can do little about them since we have no access to them. The logical extension of this theory is that what looks like conscious "choice" is really the workings of psychic forces that determine our path outside of our conscious control. The path that is "chosen" is really the path of least resistance, or least anxiety, to fulfill the primary needs of the psyche. There is a paradox of sorts, however, in this line of psychoanalytic thought; in psychoanalysis there is an assumption of the possibility for expanding the range of responses, and actually going down the path of more anxiety rather than less. Analysis assumes that the determining force can be changed, that we can be, if not totally free, at least free*er* of unconscious forces. Mitchell describes the problem thus:

> Psychodynamic motivation, according to the principle of psychic determinism, is causally closed. Within this framework the person never generates his or her own causal impact on the sequence of mental events; will and choice have no status. Freud depicts human experience as driven by forces largely unknown, a direct and unwitting product of internal pressures and compromises. Paradoxically, Freud discredits the Victorian concept of willpower, while portraying the mind as a collection of powerful willful designs and intentions; he establishes the principle of psychic determinism, while offering a treatment whose goal is the enhancement of options and responsibility.[4]

Once again the answer to paradox may lie not at one end of a polarization, but in better theorizing how both can be true at once.

There is another problem that arises given the commitment of this project to hold mind and body as coextensive and coterminously significant. The body is an "artifact" or effect of culture but can it also be a maker of culture? If increased agency is a goal for a pastoral care of resistance, something to be valued, then it cannot be relegated solely or even primarily to the psyche which would perpetuate the dualism we are seeking to avoid. Bordo reminds us that resistance is not effective

---

4. Mitchell, *Relational Concepts*, 240.

if it keeps the mind/body dualism in place or if "what the body does is immaterial, so long as the imagination is free."[5] Usually the making of culture is understood as a primarily mental activity of language and meaning making but is there a way to think of the body as a source and site of meaning and language? Once again if the body is made of culture how is it understood to also be the maker and unmaker of culture?

However, the body also cannot be that which exceeds culture or in which and through which the "real" or "true" resides. The body, though it should be understood as an agent of culture and as a source and site of agency, is also a material barrier to infinite possibility and a limitation to agency. There are limits in "sentience" but can those limits be also a resource for change? A theory of agency for resistance to the oppression operating in intimate partner violence must ask how it is that a body that is battered, a battleground, a site upon which a war is fought, can also be a sign toward hope. If subjectivity, presumed for agency, can be deconstructed through the body then it should also be able to be constructed through the body.[6]

Maureen Mahoney and Barbara Yngvesson suggest that feminists need a theory that provides an explanation of the capacity of the subject who is both creative and constrained, a "theory of active subjects who participate in the construction of the wants and needs that culture enjoins them to desire or to resist."[7] Mahoney and Yngvesson rightly suggest that explanations are needed for that which motivates persons to act in resistance as well as in conformity. What makes one of us, and not another, "want" to resist? How are *individuals* shaped in the midst of cultural prescriptions? When the discourse of agency is linked to the discourse of desire, in particular desire as constructed in object relations, the tension of the paradox is sustainable and can be identified as necessary for the presence of agency.[8]

---

5. Bordo, *Unbearable Weight*, 275.

6. This statement follows the logic of Scarry, *Body in Pain*, that we know the body makes the world by exploring how it is used to unmake the world.

7. Mahoney and Yngvesson, "Construction of Subjectivity," 44–45.

8. Mahoney and Yngvesson, "Construction of Subjectivity," makes a similar argument although they work with slightly different theory of object relations (Winnicott). Mitchell also makes a suggestion for resolution that mirrors but is not the same as the one I propose. It is beyond the scope of this volume to explore and critique these differing approaches in relation to the one being here proposed.

Construction of Agency

This chapter will show how agency emerges, albeit ambiguously, in the process of cultural construction proposed in the previous chapters. To state that culture constructs and constitutes persons is not to say that it determines them absolutely. Moreover, it is the process of construction itself that compromises the possibility of determinism and makes agency inevitable. Neither does cultural construction mean that human action is easily and infinitely revisable because it is that same process that undermines the possibility of pure freedom and restrains agency.

If the proposals made thus far in this project are accepted, agency cannot be a substantive quality of an autonomous person. Human personhood emerges out of a continuing dynamic energy that operates only through interrelatedness, a matrix of relations. Judith Butler's theory is presented here as a basis for thinking about the origins and dynamics of agency. In conjunction with the theory of persons as constructed psyche/body presented in the foregoing chapters and the theology of dynamic interrelatedness introduced in chapter two, a theological anthropology will emerge that privileges neither psyche nor body as a site of agency and which can nourish a pastoral care of resistance.

Butler's argument for agency proceeds around four points. First, she proposes that agency is not opposed to cultural construction but in fact occurs *only* because of construction and the possibility of failure in that process which is evident in culture's required continual *re*iteration. Second, the power before agency is the same power before construction, an ambiguous power (in my words the power of dynamic interrelatedness that is God) that works for both oppression and resistance; and therefore resistance is always ambivalent. Third, Butler proposes that the agency of resistance is provoked by the constitutive outside, that which is excluded and foreclosed by the law of culture and always threatens the firmness of culture's constructions. Finally, then agency must be seen as a political ascription, not a guarantee of "being" human but dependent upon one's position in the matrices of culture. The following sections explore each of these points in more detail.

The Necessity of Construction

Butler argues that, contrary to concerns to the opposite, construction enables, not forecloses, agency. To take the position that human personhood is built upon a foundational and irreducible fundamental essence, or on stable and fixed identities, is to suggest that there is someplace that remains untouchable, unchangeable and therefore must be unresponsive to resistance or any human act. Construction, on the other hand, and its posited underlying ontology of dynamic interrelatedness, opens up the possibility for acting in resistance, for changing, and at the same time it takes seriously the strong constraints upon that action. As persons we are made, built, produced, effect rather than cause and therefore able to be and act differently than before. As an emergent from an historical chain of events, persons are made but not final, enduring but revisable, and the categories by which we are defined are open to contest.

This process of cultural construction is not opposed to God, or being made by God, for if God is understood as the "organic restlessness of the web" then God may not be *the creator* but is creativity itself, that which is the power before personhood and the activity out of which and of which personhood is made. God is about action, doing, praxis, or "orthopraxis" as liberation theologians might say, and God's action is not separate from, above, or beyond human action. The activity that is God is the basis for the action that is evident in human agency. The activity, or grace of God, as wholly identified with the world, is found in the union or interrelationship and interdependence of God and persons. As Soelle says, "one has to say that God's action without us is a misunderstanding."[9] All of our activity is God's activity, and God's activity is ours.[10] There is no piece of creation that lies outside of the purview of the restlessness, the movement toward more, that is God. God is "the concrete, interconnected totality of this struggling, imperfect, unfinished, and evolving societal web."[11] God is everywhere and therefore every corner of creation is on-going and in process, not toward a specified precise goal but toward more life, new life. Persons have agency not in spite of cultural construction but because of this construction that is an outcome and ongoing creation of the dynamic power of interrelatedness that is God and the source of all action. Liberation from bondage

---

9. Soelle, *Thinking About God*, 85.

10. This is not to say that there is no activity that is not human activity for surely the earth and other creatures are also active, but this theory would suggest that the activity and energies of the non-human and humankind are deeply intertwined.

11. Loomer, "Size of God," 41.

and the accompanying increase in subjectivity will then happen only with and through the agency of persons. The quality of the relational web depends on what we do.

Once again the emphasis must shift from spatiality to temporality and from essence to energy. The activity makes the person, so that being and doing are not dichotomous but one and the same. Butler argues that there is no "'doer behind the deed,' but that the 'doer' is variably constructed in and through the deed."[12] Agency then is not rooted in a subject that had some existence and stable identity prior to or independent of the act. The structures of the psyche and the body appear as reiterated interactions and patterns of energy. The activity is not a one time event but on-going; in the psyche it can be identified as continual internalization, splitting, repression, integration and re-integration. In every moment the psyche is changing and developing, as is the body. Every aspect of the body is in constant motion, appearing as solid and fixed but in actuality shifting and changing. Bodies materialize in the repetition of activities over time. It is the action, activity, and energy of life that makes persons and are the power of human agency.

Agency cannot be rooted in a place in the subject that has remained untouched by culture or separate from the web of relations that constitutes the subject. Personhood emerges through a constructive procedure of cultural practices and meanings. Human action may appear and feel like *self*-authored, *self*-chosen action but the kind of autonomy implied in that language is but an illusion built into the process for the purpose of sustaining the prevailing rule. "No subject is its own point of departure."[13] The subjectivity of a person includes relations with others that form and constitute that person. Agency, or the "freedom"[14] to act, is not rooted in independence and separateness but in interdependence and interrelatedness. Relationality does not emerge from freedom but rather freedom emerges from relationality. Agency exists because of the

---

12. Butler, *Gender Trouble*, 142.

13. Butler, "Contingent Foundations," 9.

14. Theologically agency is often connected to discussions of "free will" as related to the human "will" to act, particularly in response to the will of God. The terms of these discussions are shifted slightly in current theological discussions of constructivism. It is beyond the scope to present and evaluate these theological issues. For brief introductions to the issues at stake in the discussion, see Bettenhausen, "Free Will"; P. Clarke, "Free Will"; Ryan, "Agency," 4–5; and for a more detailed discussion in light of feminist theory, see S. Jones. *Feminist Theory*.

dynamic interrelatedness of life itself and freedom as a quality of action emerges to a greater or lesser degree from the quality of relationship, not as a possession either self or as divine gift. Yes, there is an individual who acts and acts in particular ways specific to that individual's spirit, but it must be remembered that that individual is made of and out of a web of relations with others. Loomer puts it this way:

> Freedom, in the relational view, is a quality that belongs to the individual in his uniqueness and solitariness as it does in the traditional interpretation. But, . . . his freedom like his selfhood is an emergent from his relationships. It is peculiarly his, but it is not simply self-derived. It is a quality of his inner being, but it also reflects the world from which he emerged.[15]

The web of relations that makes up persons does not deny the uniqueness of individuals within the web but does mean, as has been demonstrated in prior chapters, that that uniqueness is held and created of others in their dynamic interrelatedness. Activity of change, the continual giving way of one moment to the next, "becomingness," Loomer reminds us, operates through equiprimordial relationship. Without interrelatedness there is no agency, no freedom to act at all. As Loomer argues:

> [The communal individual's] freedom is both his personal possession and a gift from his society. More exactly, his freedom, like his actuality, is an emergent from his relations. The community of relations includes his fellow-creatures and God. The term "relations" is a way of speaking of the presence of others in our own concrete actuality. In this conception we are related to be free, but more profoundly we are free in order to enter more fully into those relationships by which our stature is enhanced.[16]

As has been stated, in this web of restless and creative relations culture emerges as a means by which relations between persons may be maintained. The shared reality required of subjects in interaction is culture shaping the energy of psychical and material construction. The energy of change, or becoming, operates through interrelatedness, manifested in the arena of the psyche as the motivation for the estab-

---

15. Loomer, "Free and Relational Self," 73.
16. Loomer, "Theology in the American Grain," 151.

lishment and maintenance of relationship which structures the psyche of object relations. The energy that is the dynamic interrelatedness of all life is not chaotically free flowing; it is directed, albeit in multiple directions, and transformed, although within limits. While the psyche/body is indeed in constant motion, the activity is constrained and given form by the culture that forces certain compliance to norms in order to be recognized as a person, so cultural construction both enables and constrains agency. The content of intersubjective interaction, sensation, feeling, and practice are culturally determined; nevertheless there is a range of possibility for interpretation and action within any cultural situation.

Any individual act is a constituting and constructed act, but not an absolutely determined act. Butler describes, for instance, the seemingly individual act of taking of a particular theoretical position:

> My position is mine to the extent that "I"—and I do not shirk from the pronoun—replay and resignify the theoretical positions that have constituted me, working the possibilities of their convergence, and trying to take account of the possibilities that they systematically exclude. But it is clearly not the case that "I" preside over the positions that have constituted me, shuffling through them instrumentally, casting some aside, incorporating others, although some of my activity may take that form. The "I" who would select between them is always already constituted by them. The "I" is the transfer point of that replay, but it is simply not a strong enough claim to say that the "I" is situated; the "I," this "I," is *constituted* by these positions, and these "positions" are not merely theoretical products, but fully embedded organizing principles of material practices and institutional arrangements, those matrices of power and discourse that produce me as a viable "subject."[17]

Any action in the present is the effect of prior actions but in the present moment of the act the fact that it is an effect gets lost. So while it seems that we are "choosing" between, positions, for instance, the purposes, forms, limits and possibilities of the act of our choosing have already been established, and in fact made us who we are.

Subjects do act but the origin of any action is not within the subject except to the extent that we speak of the inside the subject as con-

---

17. Butler, "Contingent Foundations," 9.

structed with and of the outside. The limitations of spatial references are apparent here since the language of place, inside and outside, no longer reflects the meaning intended. It is not a place of origin that we discover but a time of origin, before and after, in relation to position. Agency originates in prior and ongoing activity. We need not assume a subject who possesses a quality, "agency," who then can act. Agency, in Butler's conjecturing, arises in the acting.

But why is it that any individual person moves in a particular direction? Each action is the result of an historical chain of previous decisions and actions. These decisions are not conscious, nor are they totally free, and they can be understood, once they have happened, by looking back at the historical progression. However, to understand reasons or motivations is not to say these motivations "caused" a person to act in a particular way but may help explain any particular action.[18] This historical chain of classification, definition, and practice or action, the terms of which are limited by culture, do not lead to only one absolutely determined action but to a range of possibilities. A person is then able, to some extent, to "choose" or coordinate the use of the tools that have been given and sometimes in quite novel ways. But any specific choice can be understood as the outcome of past choices. God is that power which provokes decision after decision, that which calls "forth more than we have been."[19]

In "Dimensions of Freedom"[20] and "The Free and Relational Self"[21] Loomer specifically addresses the question of how it is that persons are both constituted of relations and prior acts and yet are free to "decide" or "choose" acts. Loomer insists that the fact that any individual is largely "conforming" to and "reproducing" the past, the historical series of events that is synthesized in the present, does not negate the freedom of the individual person to make a unique and creative contribution to the whole of the web. Every act in the present is both provoked and dependent on the past but also "exceeds" the past. In fact the person has no choice but to *do* something, the energy must move. The "excess" or "more" may vary in degree of influence, based primarily on the position

18. See Schaefer in Mitchell and Aron, *Relational Psychoanalysis*.
19. Loomer, *Unfoldings*, 9.
20. Loomer, "Dimensions of Freedom."
21. Loomer, "Free and Relational Self," 69–86.

of the subject as will be discussed in a later section of this chapter, but that person will contribute and make a difference.

Persons make decisions about what to do with what one is given. Responsibility here is not based on what "caused" a certain action but what is done with what is.

> The self is not a complete subject who makes a decision about what it will do. The self as subject does not ontologically transcend its decision. The self is its decisions . . . The self creates itself out of what has been given to it. It is not responsible for what it has been given, as the child is not responsible for the parents who gave it birth. But the self is accountable for what it makes out of what has been given to it. Regardless of its past, its emergent self-creativity means that it must bear the onus of shaping itself. To the extent of its freedom it is responsible for being who and what it is.[22]

This is not an issue of cause or of motivation, conscious or unconscious, it is a matter of the present. A person may explore motivations and contributing factors in order to deliberate upon a choice of action but those do not change the past, assure the future or expand the range of possibilities in the present; and nevertheless the person is the one who is the outcome of those "choices." "In becoming what it in fact becomes it either adds or detracts from the qualitative richness of life."[23] And yet it cannot be forgotten that one is not infinitely or absolutely free to be whoever one wants; in fact wants, dreams, desires, and imagination are only emergents from what has already been. One is not free to "alter the conditions that set limits"[24] but one is free within those limits. Agency arises precisely because of this continual emergence, a perpetual "self-transcendence" that happens through time in the process of being constructed. The person then cannot do everything but will do something.

For any individual, the terms of that which has been, is and might be are maintained by culture. Culture accumulates the power to determine events through the practice of continually reiterated norms through a chain of citationality, in which norms gain power as they are authoritatively cited over time. Cultural construction is active, turning and returning to make the subject and because it is active, never fin-

---

22. Ibid., 75.
23. Ibid.
24. Loomer, "Dimensions of Freedom," 332.

ished, the subject is also active, agential, drawing power and direction not from outside the constituted but because of constructed constitution. Agency, then, is immanent to this process.

Ambiguous Power

The second of Butler's points about agency is that the power that energizes, enables, and provokes construction, and the determining action upon the subject by culture, also energizes, enables, and provokes agency, and the creative acting of the subject upon culture. There is one power, one impulse, one instinct, one God, of which everything is derived. This means that the power before cultural construction is paradoxically the same power before subjective agency, as is the power before oppression and resistance. This power is ambiguous, working in both what we might identify as good and as evil, thus there is a root ambivalence in any act of resistance. There is no "pure" untainted resistance but always both compliance and resistance, a tension that must be held in order for a person to be a person at all.

If, as Butler insists, "the constituted character of the subject is the very precondition of its agency,"[25] that construction is "the necessary scene of agency,"[26] then workings of culture must also be explored; for not only its determinative acting but also for the possibility of disruption. "And if there is *agency*, it is to be found, paradoxically, in the possibilities opened up in and by that constrained appropriation of the regulatory law, by the materialization of that law, the compulsory appropriation and identification with those normative demands."[27] Agency is mobilized for resistance in the reenactment of the very "law" or rules of culture we seek to resist, derived from the power of pre-existing practices. Resistance is, in a sense, already built in. Certainly we would not seek to resist a law that we did not already participate in, a law according to which we did not already act, a law to which we have already at some level conceded power. What would be the point of a movement to resist domestic violence if none of us were already participating in the cultural and personal dynamics of domestic violence? Butler is suggesting that the culture that compels us to identify and appropriate cultural

---

25. Butler, "Contingent Foundations," 12.
26. Butler, *Gender Trouble*, 147.
27. Butler, *Bodies That Matter*.

norms is also that which compels us to resist and provides the means by which we can do just that.

How does the law cited, or the power used, for subjection allow for a citation used for resistance? In every act of construction, in every reenactment of a cultural norm there lies the possibility of failure, the possibility that the norm will not hold up, that the performative will not take. The psyche is constructed through the internalization of object relations under the force of cultural norms some of which form the ego of consciousness and some that are repressed. Repression does not happen once and for all; it is a constantly reiterated event that indicates that there is constant pressure from the repressed against the force of repression. Sometimes there is slippage and repression is subverted. If this were not so there would be no need for the rules to be reiterated or for the norms to be continually symbolically re-presented. For instance, there would be no reason to continually reinforce, through language, practice, institutions, what a "good" wife is if there were no possibility of a "bad" wife. "It is this constitutive failure of the performative, this slippage between discursive command and its appropriated effect, which provides the linguistic occasion and index for a consequential disobedience."[28]

The power of dynamic interrelatedness is not unidirectional; it moves toward and away, for more and less, gives and receives, but not in just two directions on a linear plane but in multiple directions at once, thus culture moves upon and from the subject. In the tension of this twisting and turning of power through the interrelated web there is the power of the unforeseen and the "unwanted" to emerge through cracks. A particular body/psyche/person may simply raise a hand instead of her usual cowering, an unexpected, seemingly spontaneous act, that signifies a moment in time when the norm did not fully take thus revealing the possibility that things could be different than they are.

Persons develop as psyche/body in and of this ambiguous power that works both for agency and creativity and for conformity. In the body, as a site of culture and a sign of culture, there is the constant tension between sentience and subjectivity. In its ambiguity the body forces either the denial or attribution of subjectivity. The libidinal activity in and of the psyche is rooted in this tension of ambiguity at the

---

28. Ibid., 122.

heart of intersubjective construction. The other is both needed and feared, satisfying and frustrating, precisely because the other is a subject and because any development of one subject requires the presence of another subject. Thus the ambiguity itself is required, necessary to the development of a subject position, and therefore a person. The internalization, splitting and repression of the psyche are both outcomes of this ambiguity and provocation for continuing tension and ambivalence. The power out of which personhood develops leads persons to both need mutual recognition and to fear it, to do what is necessary and to resist it. Construction requires both the pressure to conform and the pressure to resist, evidenced in the psyche by the continual necessity of repeated internalization and repression. The extent to which the tension that arises out of the ambiguous power of life is either held or split, maintained or fragmented, is related to the degree of subjectivity and agency any one person can assert.

The possibility of resistance lies in the instability and incompleteness of the act of construction and subjection to culture and indicates the originating site of agency. It is not that culture has an opposing power but that culture itself is unstable and multiply directed. The power of agency is, then, also the power of cultural construction, and thus, the agency of oppression is rooted in the same power as the agency of resistance.

But how does this power turn upon itself? How does the power of subordination get reworked into the power of resistance? What happens to power and to culture in the subject that allows the subject to act against or to refuse to conform? The power that acts upon a subject is taken in and reiterated, appropriated and altered in the subject's "own" acting. To suggest that there is one power does not mean that power acts in the same way all the time, that it maintains an "identity" of sorts, which would make power a subject. Power that enables a subject's agency shifts directions, changes, never remains the same one moment to the next. In Butler's words:

> Assuming power is not a straightforward task of taking power from one place, transferring it intact, and then and there making it one's own; the act of appropriation may involve an alteration of power such that the power assumed or appropriated works against the power that made that assumption possible. Where conditions of subordination make possible the assumption of

> power, the power assumed remains tied to those conditions, but in an ambivalent way; in fact the power assumed may at once retain and resist that subordination. This conclusion is not to be thought of as (a) a resistance that is *really* a recuperation of power or (b) a recuperation that is *really* a resistance. It is both at once, and this ambivalence forms the bind of agency.[29]

Power works in different ways, through the making of the subject and in the subject's "own" making.

The alteration of power is the shift from a condition of the subject to an effect of the subject that Butler describes as two "temporal modalities" the "before" and "after" of the subject.[30] When the other is internalized as an object, for instance, power reverses and becomes an expression of the subject, but "inside," or post-internalization, the power has changed, time has elapsed. That which comes "out of" the subject while of the same energy or instinct is not exactly the same as that power was in the minute moment before, the content, form, function have been altered. Power is the prior condition that makes the subject in subjection and turns and becomes an *effect* of the subject and gives the subject a sense of agency. Agency, as an effect of the power of subjection to culture does not erase the fact that the subject then has an effect.

As described in chapter three, it is in fact the moment when power reverses, turns, when a kind of splitting takes place,[31] that the subject and its effects come into "being."

> At some point, a reversal and concealment occurs, and power emerges as what belongs exclusively to the subject (making the subject appear as if it belonged to no prior operation of power). Moreover, what is enacted by the subject is enabled but not finally constrained by the prior working of power. Agency exceeds the power by which it is enabled. One might say that the purposes of power are not always the purposes of agency. To the extent that the latter diverge from the former, agency is the assumption of a purpose *unintended* by power, one that could not have been derived logically or historically, that operates in a relation of contingency and reversal to the power that makes it possible, to which it nevertheless belongs. This is, as it were,

---

29. Butler, *Psychic Life of Power*, 13.
30. Ibid., 14.
31. Ibid., 15.

the ambivalent scene of agency, constrained by no teleological necessity.[32]

Chapter two discussed the problem of power having an aim or purpose and suggested that the only purpose of the power of dynamic interrelatedness is to keep becoming, or more life. The presumption of purpose and the paradox to which it leads binds debates about agency; but Butler's theorizing helps to open up the complicity and ambivalence at the root of agency. Every present event was only *almost* predictable, haunted by the possibility of a slip and the certainty of failure to fully take. There is no one constant aim other than to continue. While the agency of the subject exceeds construction, as the "after" of a prior event, a movement in time, it does not escape it.[33] Every act of the subject, while it may appear "new" and is in fact different, finds its energy in the "old" and acts of resistance are no exception.

Chapter two argues that ambiguity is inherent in God, the power of life, the restlessness of the web for more, and thus in human persons. God's power lies not in the aim toward good alone but in the aim toward more life in all of its fullness, which means that the full range of possibilities is open, those toward more good and toward more evil. The possibility of one requires the possibility of the other. God enables the opportunity for either but "causes" neither. Human action, as emergent from and with God's action, is always fundamentally ambivalent, reflecting the pull toward multiple directions all at once and the requirement that life itself means living in and being constituted of this ambiguous power. Culture too is made of and in this ambiguous power, working for both good and evil, for oppression and resistance.

To embrace the wholeness of God/the web/human life, means that ambiguity must be embraced. This does not mean that evil must be embraced in the sense of purposely doing evil, but rather embraced in the sense of its reality and inevitability. This kind of acknowledgement and acceptance leads to more freedom/agency/subjectivity, not less, thus the possibility of doing good, and of more life, lies not in the denial of our propensity to sin, or the power of evil available to us, but in its acknowledgement. Loomer describes it thus:

32. Ibid.
33. Ibid., 17.

> [T]he ambivalence of life, at least at the human level, is found at the core of the human spirit. On the other hand we are fearful of failure, anxious to realize our potentialities. We want the most of what life has to offer. We say that we yearn for the fullness of experience. But on the other hand we are also fearful of success. We draw back not only from the cost of success, the courage and discipline required to achieve our highest potential. We retreat also from the obligations, the challenges, and the risks that follow high achievement. The fullness of life is too much. We are afraid to die, and we are afraid to live deeply and with great openness. We would avoid the seeming nothingness of death, and yet the fullness of life seems to be too big and unmanageable. Its price is too great. We desire to be our own unique selves, and yet we want the comfort and safety of anonymity.
>
> . . . If this is so, then our psychic and spiritual ambiguities may function as forms of protection that make life possible for many or most of us.
>
> Lastly, the pervasiveness of ambiguity may be seen in contemplating the goodness and evil of a person. We cannot divide the seamless cloth of actuality, especially the concrete actuality of the self. There are no separable or autonomous divisions within the self. There is not part of the self that is the fountainhead of goodness and another part that is the ground of evil. Virtues and vices, while distinguishable in their natures, are inseparable with respect to their source. The good and evil of a person derive from the same origin. They are in fact two sides of one coin.[34]

Freedom to act, in novel ways and in resistance, is both a blessing and a curse and every human act is riddled with both; motives are always mixed; virtues can also be vices; resistance always includes complicity and is thus inevitably fraught with ambivalence.

This means that the agency required for resistance is deeply immanent to the whole web of life itself and to life lived out in concrete human history. Resistance requires a "passionate attachment" to life in all its fullness, with all of its risks and all of its possibilities for our temporal reality. The basis for resistance is not found in a transhistorical order or set of rules, or in transcendent meaning, but in the messiness and complexity of life. This action cannot be easily sorted out, categorized, or clarified. We can only continue to yearn for more than what is, keep

---

34. Loomer, "Size of God," 47.

doing the best we can with what we have, and look at the results of past actions in light of their material consequences in the present, not as a means to sort out "cause" or blame but to assess so that we can take the next ambiguous step.

Soelle's treatise on suffering points to the risks and possibilities of this approach. Suffering in and of itself simply is, an inevitable aspect of life. Human response to suffering points to a paradoxical truth that to accept suffering is to resist it when needed and transform it when possible. Soelle states:

> Every acceptance of suffering is an acceptance of that which exists. The denial of every form of suffering can result in a flight from reality in which contact with reality becomes ever thinner, ever more fragmentary. It is impossible to remove oneself totally from suffering, unless one removes oneself from life itself, no longer enters into relationships, makes one oneself invulnerable . . . The more strongly we affirm reality, the more we are immersed in it, the more deeply we are touched by these processes of dying which surround us and press upon us.[35]

It is this acceptance that enables us to "choose" suffering that meaningfully leads to more life, to just and enriched relations, and that encourages us to resist meaningless suffering which leads only to diminished life. Mutual relations will involve suffering in the interest of richer and growing relationships.

Power used unilaterally calls forth a resistance to suffering which is strengthened by our ability to fully grasp that which it is doing. "[J]ust when we come to accept that there is a suffering that makes us indestructible instead of destroying us, that teaches us to love life more than ever, that is when senseless suffering in which all these possibilities are denied, becomes visible in all its horror."[36] And yet even the distinction between the meaninglessness and meaningfulness of suffering is made not once and for all, not in ultimate clarity, but is continually worked out in the on-going history of human life. To live in passionate attachment to life is not to live in clarity but rather to take the risks involved in living fully. The capacity to feel pain is essential to feeling love.

---

35. Soelle, *Suffering*, 88.
36. Ibid., 141.

> Indifference and the possibility of getting sidetracked dare not keep us from asking about the meaning of suffering, even if we don't succeed. Not retreat from the problem, but its conquest is necessary. Improper waiting for the one who causes and takes away suffering can be overcome, and people can answer the question about suffering with their own life, which has been "conformed to the image of Christ." It is not the stoic hero who with folded arms makes himself small, waits and keeps his distance in a state of indestructibility; it is not he who shows the possibility for humanizing suffering. Rather it is the mystic sufferer who opens his hands for everything coming his way. He has given up faith in and hope for a God who reaches into the world from outside, but not hope for changing suffering and learning from suffering.[37]

The agency need for resistance is found not in denial of limitations but in embrace; not in absolute freedom but in the ambiguous freedom of created and creating, constituted and constituting subjects; not in an abstract God who will act on our behalf or give us absolute and unchanging rules to live by, but in God as the dynamic power of interrelatedness in *all* that is.

In order to find signs of hope, where does the "mystic" who opens to everything in all its ambiguities look? Where does one go? At what point in time and space does resistance happen and how? Soelle turns to the marginalized and oppressed, Butler to the "constitutive outside." That which is denied, repressed, unknown, excluded will push for recognition, rattle the edges, threaten the status quo, provoke a new idea or feeling or practice, assure the ever-presence of resistance and be a sign to that which will increase the fullness of life and stature of all.

Constitutive Outside

The third point in Butler's theorizing about agency is that agency used for resistance is provoked and evidenced by the constitutive outside. This project is concerned about agency in as much as it is a necessary prerequisite for resistance. It is the "capacity" to act in resistance to oppression and abuse that is of interest to practitioners of pastoral care in the context of intimate partner violence. Cultural construction enables agency by virtue of its dynamic and interrelated character. The

37. Ibid., 144–45.

power that sustains and enables both construction by and of culture and agency in and of the subject twists and turns in its movement such that construction in the normalizing mode of culture will be both reiterated and resisted. There is not one act of construction but an ongoing activity in which power works both for maintaining norms and for resisting and changing those norms. This power is thus ambiguous and all actions of resistance are thus performed with core ambivalence, rooted in both our desire to be recognized and our desire for more life. As noted above, the question arises: how, in this paradoxical ambiguous ambivalence, is resistance to be understood and even pursued? How is resistance to be identified such that agency might be thus used? Where there is construction, which is to say, where there is power, there is resistance but where is it located, when does it happen, and can we do more of it if we want to? Butler suggests that in looking to the "constitutive outside" resistance becomes apparent.

Any invocation of a category, or a conventional practice, involves setting the boundaries for what falls into that category and what does not. Both the inside *and* the outside are required, thus the "outside" is "constitutive" of the inside and at the same time opens that category to contest from that which the category fails to represent. The "constitutive outside," is excluded, foreclosed, eclipsed in the citation, but not eradicated, absent but not destroyed. Those exclusions will haunt the edges of the categorization. Those edges are the site of resistance. There lies the persistent possibility of disruption. In those moments of turning a space is opened up, a slight moment in time for something slightly different to occur, for the outside to slip in, or at least make a momentary appearance. For instance, as Butler points out, when the category "woman" is contested for its error of universality, new possibilities emerge. Butler suggests that political efficacy resides precisely in the exclusions that are presumed by any totalizing category. At the limits of its generalizability "woman" is revealed as a performative masquerading as description and representation and thus also reveals the possibility that the category can be changed.

As the subject is formed in the process of assuming the norms of culture, a disidentification also occurs and produces that which is rejected, not assumed, what Butler calls "abjects."[38]

38. Butler, *Bodies that Matter*, 12; Benjamin, *Shadow of the Other* (101–3), critiques Butler's notion of abjects, questioning how they can be active and influential if they are

> The abject designates here precisely those "unlivable" and "uninhabitable" zones of social life which are nevertheless densely populated by those who do not enjoy the status of the subject, but whose living under the sign of the "unlivable" is required to circumscribe the domain of the subject. This zone of uninhabitability will constitute the defining limit of the subject's domain; it will constitute the site of dreaded identification against which —and by virtue of which—the domain of the subject will circumscribe its own claims to autonomy and to life. In this sense, then, the subject is constituted through the force of exclusion and abjection, one which produces a constitutive outside to the subject, an abjected outside, which is, after all "inside" the subject as its own founding repudiation.[39]

The construction of the subject occurs in a process of selectivity, a continual marking off, of abstracting or bringing to the foreground some while denying others. Resistance involves challenging those markings from within its own "logic." Abjects, not to be understood as other subjects or as positions but as "discursive possibilities,"[40] materialize subject/bodies/persons and force the continual *re*articulation and the possibility of change.

In the psyche it is the unconscious, as that which is split off, repressed, unthinkable and unknowable, the constitutive outside of the psyche, and its constant pressure and influence that both forces rearticulation and allows and locates the possibility of resistance and change. An act of resistance will come from the inseparability of the conscious and unconscious, not as a purely conscious act but as an ambiguous act in which both the disallowed and the allowed will negotiate for expression. In the continual reiteration of repression and its limits and failures, that which is repressed can appear like a spectre at the edges of the psyche or can find its way through the barrier in a minute moment in time and thus operate as a site and sign of resistance. In the body the same kind of dynamics are happening as the ambiguity and tensions of bodily sentience and subjectivity are competing, defining and mapping

---

not subjects. As I read Butler, Benjamin may be confusing abjects with persons rather than understanding them as discursive events. Benjamin does make a good point that exclusion may be better described as "relocation." Something must be present, even if only in imagination, in order to be excluded.

39. Butler, *Bodies That Matter*, 3.
40. Ibid., 12.

the body. When the body "acts up" or "acts out" and the unthinkable is done or when sensation arises in the most "inappropriate" time and place, the norms are revealed for what they are, historical constructions of the culture put forth by the ruling hegemony. At these points in time the way of resistance is revealed, not as unambiguous, but as resistance nevertheless.

It is in the failure of what is proclaimed as descriptive and in the incoherence of that which is deemed meaningful that the agency for resistance arises. When women's lives appear unreal and fail to fit into the prevailing descriptions and meanings of violence, love, passion, discipline, sex, rape, wife, or marriage; when they appear as inconceivable contradiction, they also reveal the agency of resistance. When the home is described as and presumed to be a "safe haven" resistance occurs at the point of denial—that the home is the most dangerous place for women. In the subversion of the category—safe home—political change happens not only by subversion but also by the potential for resignification or changing the meaning of "home," even if ever so slightly. And as the battered women's movement picked up the slogan "every home a safe home"[41] it subverted the prevailing idea(l) of home, named that which was denied in the ideal, and yet derived power from the norm of an ideal which desired home as a "safe" (and private) place; thus it temporarily left in place the patriarchal ideology's notions of home and family until that assumption was then challenged. As Butler points out, "this turning of power against itself to produce alternative modalities of power, to establish a kind of political contestation that is not a 'pure' opposition, but a difficult labor of forging a future from resources inevitably impure."[42] The constitutive outside should not be interpreted as the outside of culture but rather a creation of culture and a necessity for cultural construction.

If God is the whole of the world, the totality of the cosmos, the restless web of interrelatedness in which we live and move and have our being, then this outside that constitutes the inside is also in and of God. As it continually moves toward more life, the web ambiguously brings with it both the possibility for more good, increased stature/subjectivity, and for more evil, decreased stature/subjectivity. Resistance to evil

41. This is a slogan used for many years by the National Coalition Against Domestic Violence.

42. Butler, *Bodies That Matter*, 241.

involves embracing the whole of God, not an unambiguous "perfect" God but an ambiguous one. To embrace ambiguity means to not abstract from context, whether in reference to thought, feeling, sensation, etc. Union with God as an attachment to or immersion in the whole of life suggests that resistance might be located in relationships themselves as they negotiate the pull to abstraction from the whole and the tie to the fullness of the context. Loomer states:

> [N]either self-consciousness nor knowledge can provide an adequate directive for the reformation of society or the evolution of the human spirit. They can provide the conditions that can facilitate or frustrate the working of the directive, but the directive is to be found within those processes involved in sustained, mutually internal relations. The "wisdom" that can be trusted, and the kind of power consistent with this wisdom, are contained within, or emerge from, these relationships.[43]

"Sustained mutually internal relations" require an outside and a continual confrontation with the outside, a continual reiteration or renegotiation of the outside and inside. The wisdom of God directs us to the contrasts and contradictions, to the edges of what we think are the possibilities, to the impossible, and the extent to which they are indeed possible. Transformation of the world occurs as "incompatibilities and contradictions" are included as "compatible contrasts within the unity of the web and within the lives of its members."[44]

Resistance then may be known through unusual paths, by being deeply involved in the whole of the world, and the whole of our own personhood, that which is readily abstracted and that which seems to remain in the background of the unknown and unexpereinced. As Loomer says, "This is where God, envisioned as the web, is most powerfully and profoundly at work."[45] Loomer suggests that this kind of involvement in the world will perhaps require more "non-cognitive forms of awareness, in contrast to sensory and rational methods of relating to our environment."[46] The need for resistance, the mode of resistance, and the agency for resistance are opened up at these liminal edges of life.

---

43. Loomer, "Size of God," 30.
44. Ibid., 51.
45. Loomer, "On Committing Yourself to a Relationship," 260.
46. Ibid., 261.

In the concrete context of culture structured in and by norms of acceptability established by the currently more powerful, these edges demarcating that which is inside and outside can be found where those who are excluded and denied subjectivity, where embodied "abjects" trying to become subjects, are located. The marginalized, not unambiguously so, expose the limits of construction, the necessity for resistance, and the way in which resistance happens. In God's on-going creativity those on the margins can suggest the path toward more life, a larger embrace of the whole. Immersion into the depths and breadths of the world will lead us not only to the beauty of life, but also to the suffering of life, they are of one another.[47] To attach to, delve into, embrace and immerse ourselves in the world is to both seek and discover union with God in all God's fullness and will inevitably require a growing awareness that the suffering of the victims, the unattended to, the unknown, of our culture is also our own suffering. This situation demands a response. It is here that we find the strength to "choose life," as Soelle puts it.[48] "The poor are the teachers," she says.[49] In them we find faith and hope and the agency of resistance to the aspects of culture that are life diminishing and damaging to mutual relationship. Victims of cultural hegemonies are the constitutive outside of the privileged, and though the privileged believe they can have life in spite of or irrespective of the poor they are in fact dying along with them. According to Soelle, we learn of resistance to meaningless suffering through participation in the suffering of the oppressed, as one is freed from bondage, increased in subjectivity, so are all. We go to the edges, to the boundaries, those places and peoples and experiences we have not dared to acknowledge and find the creative activity of God for more life.

However, the "poor" are not pure. They are part of the whole, made in the ambiguous power of God. As persons they are more or less subjects, not fully "abjects." Their resistance must involve some complicity, some recognition of the "game," some concession to the values, otherwise why would anyone want to move from the outside to the inside. Although the constitutive outside can provoke novelty, creativity, and transformation it does so under the constraints of culture. While we

---

47. Soelle, *Silent Cry*.
48. Soelle, *Choosing Life*.
49. Soelle, *Thinking About God*, 19.

can learn, plan and organize for resistance we cannot be sure of the effects of any act. One can use the tools at hand, look to the sites of contradiction and exclusion, and yet still resistance will always also be complicity and the effects will always be unpredictable. "For one is, as it were, in power even as one opposes it, formed by it as one reworks it, and it is this simultaneity that is at once the condition of our partiality, the measure of our political unknowingness, and also the condition of action itself. The incalculable effects of action are as much a part of their subversive promise as those that we plan in advance."[50]

Political Ascription

The political nature of agency brings us to the fourth point in this excursus. Agency as an outcome of the cultural construction of subjectivity means that it, the acting of a subject, does not have an ontological "existence." Agency is constructed in and of the power that energizes and structures that same construction. There is no guaranteed agency that is part and parcel of being human, and especially no guarantee of a certain "equal dose" for every person. Every person can act or "has" agency but only to the extent that she or he is recognized as a subject under the current regulations and then only to the extent allowed by those regulations. Agency is then born in the politics of power, the manner in which the power of interrelatedness is used for the rule of relationships as they intersubjectively produce subjects. Butler states:

> But if we agree that politics and power exist already at the level at which the subject and its agency are articulated and made possible, then agency can be *presumed* only at the cost of refusing to inquire into its construction. Consider that "agency" has no formal existence or, if it does, it has no bearing on the question at hand. In a sense, the epistemological model that offers us a pregiven subject or agency is one that refuses to acknowledge that *agency is always and only a political prerogative*. As such it seems crucial to question the conditions of its possibility, not to take it for granted as an a priori guarantee.[51]

Every subject, due to its constructed and culturally constituted nature and its assignment to a subject position, has agency, not as a possession

---

50. Butler, *Bodies That Matter*, 241.
51. Butler, "Contingent Foundations," 13.

but rather as an action or event, or rather a series of events, a citational legacy or reference to, concession to, and reiteration of "laws" or norms that make subjects. However, the degree of agency, the intensity and influentiality, is, like subjectivity itself, a "political prerogative." Agency cannot be presumed; it happens at the discretion of the governing norms, institutions, practices, and language.

The structures of power ascribe agency according to the rules of those who rule which makes it a political action. But of course, to identify the political is also to identify the personal—the two are of the same fabric. Personal agency is political; therefore the agency needed for resistance is greater for some than for others. Position in relation to the web of relations is crucial to assessing agency and the possibility for resistance; and therefore crucial to a pastoral care that hopes to foster resistance to intimate partner violence and the cultural injustices that psychically/materially/ spiritually maintain it. This position should not be understood in static or spatial terms but as a discursive position, multiple, dynamic and ambiguous, a temporal position, a moment in time in which the dynamic and creative power of interrelatedness concresces in a certain structural moment that is at once repeating the past and becoming something new.

If agency is not to be taken for granted as guaranteed then it must be seen as regulated. In the interest of political and personal resistance, the concern for ministers of pastoral care is the means by which agency is fostered so that it might be turned for resistance to that which is ultimately life diminishing. The question to be asked of agency is about how it is produced in the practices of culture. Butler continues:

> We need instead to ask, what possibilities of mobilization are produced on the basis of existing configurations of discourse and power? Where are the possibilities of reworking that very matrix of power by which we are constituted, of reconstituting the legacy of the constitution, and of working against each other those processes of regulation that can destabilize existing power regimes? For if the subject is constituted by power, that power does not cease at the moment the subject is constituted, for that subject is never fully constituted, but is subjected and produced time and again. That subject is neither a ground nor a product, but the permanent possibility of a certain resignifying process, one which gets detoured and stalled through other

mechanisms of power, but which is power's own possibility of being reworked.[52]

These tasks of resignification, dis-identification, destabilization, of fostering agency for resistance, are then political tasks and as such make acts of pastoral care also always political. They will reiterate and may resist the rules of the game for what it means to be "persons" in any particular moment.

If agency is evident in the possibility of failure in the constitutive reiteration of norms, and if the undergirding power of this constructive process is the same as that which can work against this process or to some extent refuse to comply with it, and if the constitutive outside not only reveals the construction but points to the site of resistance to that construction, and if it is then clear that agency is a political event, the question arises: how can resistance become a strategized event? Butler suggests that, "The critical task is, rather, to locate strategies of subversive repetition enabled by those constructions, to affirm the local possibilities of intervention through participating in precisely those practices of repetition that constitute identity and, therefore, present the immanent possibility of contesting them."[53] In other words, since resistance cannot be thought of outside the culture that constructs us, it must be thought of *inside* the culture. The idea is to play on that which is proclaimed as unconstructed, to use the strength of the reiteration and its historical legacy to turn the performance on itself and thus reveal it for what it is.

As Butler illustrates, the parody of drag reveals gender as a performance; the appropriation of the identification "queer" by the very persons it is meant to insult reduces the power of the slur precisely because of its historical interpretation. No one is supposed to want to be called "queer." When the "unnatural" is engaged[54] to reveal the "natural" for the "fictions of power" that they are, the power of those fictions is at least slightly reduced and shifted.[55] When a heretofore "passive" victim,

---

52. Ibid.
53. Butler, *Gender Trouble*, 147.
54. Ibid., 149.
55. For a critique of Butler on this point see Bordo, *Unbearable Weight*, 289–90, who raises the question: who decides whether or not and to what extent an act, such as drag, is subversive?

like Rodriguez, picks up a two-by-two and whacks her abusive partner who is trying to "teach her a lesson" she reveals that she has indeed learned a lesson and reveals the intended lesson for what it is. This is not a "pure subversion"[56] in the sense that it does not completely and absolutely subvert or negate the power of the cultural hegemonic norm, and may in fact leave in place much of the historically developed and powerful legacy, but it is nevertheless a shift, a movement against that which has been. The woman with the two-by-two has used violence to resist violence which leaves in place the norm of violence but at the same time challenges the norms by which violence is understood. The fact that the resources are inevitably "impure" does not mean that they are totally ineffectual.

Additionally the effects of resistance, because of the instability and ongoing dynamic of power, cannot be wholly predicted and calculated. They can be strategized and planned, and given the familiarity with the "rules of the game," somewhat or partially predicted but there is always also the possibility of failure, of incompleteness, of disruption and interruption by the foreclosed, that which even the best laid plans failed to take into account. As Butler points out, "The incalculable effects of action are as much a part of their subversive promise as those that we plan in advance."[57] The fact that resistance is always also fraught with complicity, that it is always ambivalent, and may raise more problems than it solves, does not mean that it should not be done or that the "impure" that has been done is somehow invalid. It simply suggests that any act of resistance will open up new possibilities for further resistance.

The political nature of human agency also demands that any fostering of resistance requires a careful analysis of the structures and workings of power in and through culture, using the tools at hand to chip away at that which those tools have built. The norms by which psyches/bodies are split and mapped can be assessed and evaluated. The regulations that determine what will be split and repressed, what will and will not be done, or what and when one will feel what one feels can be explored. The assessments will be limited and incomplete, perhaps only temporarily relevant and effective; nevertheless they will matter.

---

56. Butler, *Bodies That Matter*, 240.
57. Ibid., 241.

The criteria by which these evaluations will be made can be found in the theological commitments expressed throughout this project.

Throughout this thesis the norm by which an act is judged for its value is the degree to which any act uses the power of dynamic interrelatedness, which is God, for more life or not. How does an act enrich and strengthen the web of relations or does it weaken them? How does the act work for increased subjectivity and liberation or diminishment thereof? It is not that there are clear unambiguous certain answers to these questions but that within the web itself direction will be indicated. The power of the web can be used unilaterally for control of one by another and mutually for expanded and enriched relationship. These uses of power, as they are reiterated and repeated patterns of relating, become the sociocultural structures of the web and thus politically charged. Divine/human agency is then a deeply political matter. As Soelle puts it, the question that must be asked of suffering is: whom does it serve?[58] Agency is a matter of political struggle over who is controlled by whom; whose actions are recognized and whose are not; who defines the meaning of any act and who will have influence on the actions of another. Fostering and mobilizing agency for resistance requires political struggle because it is politics that determines what gets repressed, what sentience gets denied, and what practices must be disallowed. A pastoral care of resistance will then require political analysis, struggle and action. Increased subjectivity and liberation are, as Soelle says, "total concepts":

> [B]y total I mean one with different physical and spiritual dimensions. Where liberation takes place, one can see how people change: in their bodies, in their relationships to one another, in their social relationships; how their neighborhood, their streets, their schools, take on another appearance. In this sense liberation is a change of the whole of life, of life-style, of behaviour.[59]

All pastoral care is political activity; the question that must be asked is "whom does it serve?"

Soelle also calls for the maintenance of a "fighting spirit" that "gives up the constant toleration of injustice, this helpless, self-pitying

---

58. Soelle, *Suffering*, 134–35.
59. Soelle, *Thinking About God*, 88.

'We can't do anything about it' position."[60] Anyone who is a person can, and inevitably will, do something. Political structures, practices and meaning-making will allow some to do more than others but the key for pastoral care is to assess, given what is, how much agency any particular person is likely to be able to mobilize for that which will bring more life, more freedom. Freedom emerges from dynamic interrelatedness and is enhanced by power used for mutuality, not the other way around. The minister of pastoral care must also then assess her or his own contribution to, in complicity and resistance, the reigning hegemonic norms.

Summary

This proposal for a way of thinking about agency addresses the issues raised in the introduction to this chapter. Agency as both enabled and constrained by culture and its construction of subjects, suggests that while there are victims of culture these victims are also agents of culture. Agency is neither denied nor fully free. To be constructed of culture is to be able to resist that culture, since the agency to resist is derived of the same power as the culture that constrains. Persons may "choose" to act but the limits of choice are set by cultural practices, institutions, language, and meaning, often *un-* or *sub-* consciously performed. They are not totally free but not fully determined either. Responsibility and accountability cannot be linked in this instance to cause but rather must be understood in terms of current assignments of agency by the cultural milieu. Some are allowed more subjectivity than others and the extent to which they are allowed will have more influence and more possibility to resist than others. Any individual's possibility for acting in resistance will reside in her or his particular history and context, some of which may be shared with others but also individually determined, and will also always be ambiguously as both victim and agent of culture.

Paradoxically the most victimized, the constitutive outside if you will, as in victims of intimate partner violence, may suggest the clearest path to understanding agency and the mobilization of it for resistance. The victims are the teachers. Agency is constructed, ambiguous in nature, and always politically ascribed. Resistance then is never pure, never fully against the prevailing culture, and yet real and active nevertheless. Out of the midst of these ambiguous and constantly shifting terrains,

---

60. Ibid., 88–89.

pastoral care in the interest of resistance to useless suffering will forge out of ambivalent desires partial and temporary paths to healing and more life.

6

A Pastoral Care For Resistance

THE PURPOSE OF THIS BOOK HAS BEEN TO RESPOND TO QUESTIONS THAT arise as the tensions between persons as victims and agents of culture are considered, especially in the context of intimate partner violence. Ministers of pastoral care are concerned with the suffering of particular persons and with the amelioration of that suffering. If suffering is understood in terms of victimization, in the case of intimate partner violence victimization by an oppressive culture, then resistance to that culture is essential for the mitigation of that suffering. Chapter one pointed out, however, that victims of intimate partner violence were both victims and resisters or agents of culture and of their lives. Victims do resist and agents are also victims. As the exploration of this tension has unfolded it has become clear that victimization and agency, including the agency to resist, work in concert with each other, and both are outcomes of cultural construction. It has been demonstrated in the preceding chapters that persons can be identified as victims *and* agents when understood as radically culturally constructed. The boundaries between internal and external are called into question since psyche/body/culture are identified as made of and by each other. Agency arises in that construction, not as the self-determined action of an autonomous subject but as the ambiguous working of the dynamic power of interrelatedness that both constrains and enables the activity of the subject.

The preceding chapters have offered a theory/theology of the cultural construction of human personhood and agency that makes sense given the experience of caring with and for victims of intimate partner violence. But this is not sufficient for ministers of pastoral care whose interest it is to bring this new understanding back to the practice of responding with care to human suffering in particular human persons. This theological anthropology must inform a practice of care that can assist in the healing and liberating of "real" hurting persons. This exploration into agency was undertaken with the intent not only of learning about and understanding the dynamics of agency but specifically so that the agency of resistance might be fostered in order to limit, if not eradicate, meaningless suffering. This chapter returns the focus to intimate partner violence and asks how we might use what victims themselves have suggested to us about agency for more subjectivity and liberation. How can ministers of pastoral care foster the agency needed for resistance to that which diminishes life for victims of intimate partner violence? What can be done in the relationship between victim and pastoral care provider to increase agency and resistance given the theological anthropology presented in this book?

This chapter will focus on the concrete implications of the theology of agency presented in the preceding chapters for a pastoral care for resistance with victims of intimate partner violence. The discussion will once again revolve around the four foci offered in chapter five. Agency for resistance can be fostered in as much as it is recognized to arise from the cultural construction of human personhood and the possibility of its failure; as emergent from the ambiguous power that energizes both oppression and resistance and therefore is always ambivalent; sought at the boundaries of the constitutive outside, and dependent upon political prerogatives. I present four related strategies for a pastoral care for resistance.

Attachment to the Now and the More

Agency is a product of the cultural construction and constitution of human personhood that works through the dynamic interrelatedness that is the whole web of life. A pastoral care of resistance will encourage a passionate attachment to the present as it is constructed of the past and to the more that is the constant restlessness of the web. Many texts on intimate partner violence recommend safety and story-telling as initial steps of response.[1] The theory/theology of construction that I have proposed suggests that the present moment is full in and of itself; it is both brought forth from the past but is also full of creativity and infinite

1. See, for instance, Eugene and Poling, *Balm for Gilead*; Herman, *Trauma and Recovery*; and Neuger, *Counseling Women*.

possibility. The provision of relative[2] safety for the victim is based on the realities of the present, not on what might come of that for the future or on what may or may not have been done in the past. This does not mean that information about past occurrences or evaluation of likely consequences in the future does not affect what is done in the present. It does mean that now is sufficient. For victims of intimate partner violence this may mean going to shelter for the tenth time; it may mean an hour at a friend's or with a pastor; it may mean compliance with the demands of the batterer (even that can mean more safety in the moment than trying to fight back). The point is that the past cannot be changed and the future cannot be predicted; the present is sufficient basis upon which to form an action.

While not absolutely determined by the past, any action in the present relies on the past and emerges from past experience and the meanings attached to those experiences. Often a bit of relative safety opens up the space for reflection or story-telling,[3] a narrative that gives meaning to the present in light of the past. The story-telling, however, is not a full record of history as it was but rather as it is. In the present telling of the story construction of the present and the future is continued. The narrative is itself an immersion in the on-going construction of personhood. This recitation of history reveals the complex factors that bring the victim and the minister of pastoral care to this point and is reconstructing and reframing the events of the past in light of the current interaction and situation. With each new experience another piece of the story is added or altered.

A return to the autobiography of Stephanie Rodriguez helps illustrate this point. Rodriguez's first version of her life story was four pages long and entitled "Better Off Godless."[4] Later when she looked at the story again more complexity was added; she found "new villains" and "new people and things to blame."[5] In her preface she writes:

---

2. Given the interrelatedness of reality and the construction of that reality by hegemonic norms there is no "truly" safe place only places of relatively less or more safety.

3. Neuger, *Counseling Women*, speaks of "coming to voice" and echoes several of the points I am making here.

4. Rodriguez, *Time to Stop Pretending*, 11–15.

5. Ibid., 17.

> Getting into the whole ugly mess in the first place hadn't just happened, though. That's what this book is about—how I got into it, and what it was like.
>
> I've told the story in small pieces, each of which stresses a particular point important to an understanding of the abuse. In the process, I have found, I think, a larger truth. I find that my husband didn't do what he did to me by himself. He had plenty of help. His parents, my parents, our society all worked together. They set us up, from the start, to become the abuser and the abused.[6]

The story is constructed and reconstructed and so is her life. At each point of reflection new pieces of the construction and the interrelatedness of all those pieces become apparent. It is in this immersion into constructive process that the minister of pastoral care and the victim will tell a new story each adding pieces. In the interest of resistance it is crucial to tie the individual experiences to the cultural dynamics, noting the means by which thoughts, values, and feelings, psychodynamic and material life, are culturally prescribed in order to keep a certain order or rule. Domestic violence then is revealed as an outcome of the intersection of personal, cultural, and political, a flaw in the whole that deeply affects each and every part, or each and every individual.

As several theorists point out[7] it is vital, however, that well-intentioned pastoral caregivers do not try to simplify the complexity and particularity of the victim's story, as an abstraction from the richness of context that will diminish agency. As Elizabeth Schneider reminds us, the particularity of women's experience can be placed in the more general story of women's subordination but the general will be experienced in very individual ways. It can be tempting, especially with a little education on the subject, for pastoral care providers to operate from a pre-conceived notion of who battered women are and how domestic violence happens. It is more helpful to be open to that which does not fit the current theory but is the "reality" of a woman's life as she understands it.

The present state of things is a result of a complex convergence of factors. But in the revelation of the construction is also hope, since

---

6. Ibid., 8–9.

7. Mahoney and Yngvesson, "Construction of Subjectivity," 44; Schneider, "Particularity and Generality."

what has been constructed can be deconstructed and reconstructed. As a story-teller of the faith, the minister of pastoral care will also offer a version of the story as told in relation to the divine and a pastoral care of resistance will then be intentional about the way that the God narrative either fosters or diminishes agency for fuller life. I have offered one such narrative in which God is identified as the "organic restlessness" of life when life is understood as operating through interrelatedness.

The passionate attachment to the now is also a commitment to the more, inherent in the dynamic interrelatedness that is life itself. The web of life in which we live and move and have our being is naturally always becoming something more, moving in time, accumulating past experience into the present moment and always moving beyond that moment to the next. At the heart of life is activity and creativity moving through this web of relations through time and space. This means that nothing is set in stone, so to speak, that change is inevitable and that there is within persons always a yearning for more life. Living fully in the present reveals this yearning and enables more agency or capacity to act for more, as the scriptures say, "abundant" life.[8]

This attachment to the now, to the situation at hand, and to the more of life can, as I have put forth in this book, be understood as attachment to God. This perspective is indicated by Rodriguez's words:

> I grew away from my god. The further I got from him, the closer I got to myself and my family, to reality. The less I depended on him, the more I depended on me. I even decided that paradise could wait, at least until I got my kids grown. They needed me. I was quicker to action on their behalf than was God. I didn't know why.[9]

Her reflection suggests that a God who is identified with reality could be understood to foster the agency for resistance.[10] Rodriguez initially understood her husband's beatings as part of God's plan for her life; she states, "I didn't know why God wanted me beat up, but considering

---

8. John 10:10.

9. Rodriguez, *Time to Stop Pretending*, 15.

10. It should be noted that it is clearly my own agenda as a pastoral theologian to make theological sense out of Rodriguez's words. I am not suggesting that she should follow my suggestion, nor am I suggesting that her own interpretation, repudiating God altogether, is not valid for her. My interest is in finding theological language that makes sense in light of and can, with some integrity, stand next to Rodriguez's story.

his Joan of Arc plan, I guess I thought myself pretty lucky."[11] This kind of god-language constructs a god who is oriented not to the present and to the fullness of life in the now but toward the future. It was when Rodriguez went against the "silly plan"[12] that she was able to find more agency and to resist. I am suggesting that God can be understood as that which provokes the going againstness, the yearning for more life in the present and the creative and on-going activity of life itself. Rodriguez states that, "I was quicker to action on their behalf than was God"; and I have proposed that her action can be thought of as empowered by God's action that is the basis for all action. God is that which continually calls forth more, more activity, more life, not out of a transcendent order but out of the dynamic interrelatedness in which and from which all persons are made. In her initial brief story Rodriguez closes with the statement, "I don't wait for God to do anything anymore, and nobody ever hits us."[13] We do not have to wait, God is acting now through us and with us.

None of this, however, should be understood as a turn to human free will in the sense of unconstrained freedom to do what we want. Victims of intimate partner violence make it clear that freedom and possibility are complexly limited in this web of relatedness, and that while God is forever active and moving, God is also holding back and restricting that activity. Victims face both external—force, economic dependence, lack of community assistance—and internal—fear, commitments to certain values, lack of ego strength, bodily dissociation—restraints and the two are constructed by each other. Freedom emerges from interrelatedness and more so from the power of interrelatedness used for mutuality. The relationship of victim and minister of pastoral care, in as much as it is grounded in mutuality, will provide a framework for increased agency. That relationship ideally offers the constraints, boundaries and creativity needed for agency and thus resistance to grow.

The activity of construction is a process of being constituted of an historical chain of "decision" about what is done. Subjects, victims, have been acting and will act; the question is how each act is "chosen" or "decided." These decisions are made unconsciously, subconsciously, and

---

11. Rodriguez, *Time to Sop Pretending*, 12.
12. Ibid., 14.
13. Ibid., 15.

consciously but all are both individual and cultural, not self-authored, in the sense of a self that is an autonomous being. The terms of decision and choice are set, determined, not so that the victim has only one option but that the experience of choice, both in terms of possibility and limits, is constructed by culture in both its external and internal dynamics.

A pastoral care of resistance will take seriously the ways in which choice is constructed. For instance, when a victim voices her desire to return home to the batterer, agency will be limited if the pastoral caregiver suggests that what she "really" wants is something else and it is only cultural patriarchy that says return *is* what she wants to do. In fact the culture of patriarchy is "really" her and is what gives ministers the idea that they somehow know better what is going on than the victim. At the same time the complex dynamic of internal/external construction must be remembered. As Hirschmann points out, our concept of choice is overly individualized and must be reconsidered from a "conception of freedom [that] requires us to acknowledge how external factors influence and generate inner feelings and motives, as well as how those inner feelings act on and influence the external world."[14] She then goes on to say, "Women are not responsible for their battering. But they are responsible for and to themselves."[15] They are not responsible for what has been given to them or what has brought them to any particular point in time but they are responsible for what they do in that moment given the possibilities and constraints provided. The role of the minister of pastoral care is then to enter into a relationship that might clarify and expand the terms of those choices in the hope that the victim's choice can be as "authentic"[16] as it can be in the current historical moment. The choice is only theirs to make, however limited or ambiguous the terms of that choice may be, which brings us to the next point for a pastoral care of resistance.

Acknowledgment and Acceptance of Ambiguity

The power before agency is both the power used for constraint, and injustice, and the power used for creativity, and resistance to injustice. A

14. Hirschmann, "Theory and Practice of Freedom," 206.
15. Ibid.
16. See Mitchell, *Relational Concepts*, 9, referred to in chapter 3.

pastoral care of resistance will acknowledge and accept the ambiguity at the root of this power and the resulting core ambivalence at the heart of resistance. Acts of resistance are always to some degree also acts of complicity with that which one is resisting; to deny this ambiguity is to deny agency and decrease subjectivity. Rodriguez's description of the night she "picked up the two-by-two" is an illustration of this ambiguous reality.

> A quick "whack" from the two-by-two stopped it, right then. Just like that, it ended. No praying or waiting for a disinterested god to take action. I did it myself with one quick whack.
> Unfortunately, I couldn't muster another. I dropped the board; he picked it up. The rest of the night was pretty messy. It involved emergency people. But a change had begun.[17]

She picked up the board and hit him with a "quick whack."[18] She used the tools of her batterer husband, the board and hitting, as an act of resistance, of refusal to comply, and yet it was also compliance since her act reiterated the norms for power used through weapons and acts of hitting to make one's self known. In this case the power of oppression was turned against itself, not completely but sufficiently enough to reveal the possibility that something different might be possible. The power of "his" act turned when it was enacted by her, not that she had a revelation or found power from outside the context but that within the context existed the power for resistance as well as for abuse. Following her act, he picked up the board and the "rest of the night was pretty messy."[19] He was not yet in *total* control over her. The failure of the reiteration of oppression and abuse revealed by Rodriguez's own acting necessitates further continual reiteration by the batterer but also makes apparent the way in which this unilateral use of power works in the construction of this relationship and these two participants for control and coercion and for the possibility of resistance. As Rodriguez states it, "a change had begun."[20]

17. Rodriguez, *Time to Stop Pretending*, 14.
18. Ibid.
19. Ibid.
20. Ibid.

A pastoral care of resistance will acknowledge the forging of a future "out of impure resources"[21] and will consider the complex context of dynamics at play as the caregiver and victim seek to increase agency in the identification of resistance and seek also to carry out acts of resistance. In the context of intimate partner violence acts of resistance are many more than leaving the household or terminating the relationship.[22] As Gondolph reminds us, victims act in resistance from the very beginning and usually increase that resistance as abuse intensifies.[23] These acts of resistance can include everything from compliance with demands in order to avoid a worse beating to acts of violence in fighting back. These acts reveal the victim's agency as present to some extent except in the most extreme conditions of torture. As Mahoney suggests, agency and victimization are not known by the absence of the other and "we need strategies that reveal both agency and oppression and facilitate resistance."[24] She then suggests two such strategies: challenge to the concept that agency is synonymous with exit from the relationship and maintaining the concept of battering as a pattern of power and control rather than looking at discrete acts of violence.

In the interest of increased agency, the minister of pastoral care will do well to acknowledge the ambivalence present in the psyches and bodies of victims and realize that an acceptance of ambivalence, rather than pushing for unambivalent clarity, is necessary in order to move toward more liberation. This means, for instance, to listen to the mixed motivations and desires, including the desire to leave and to stay, to keep the relationship and not to be battered. It may mean also remembering that the intersubjective construction of personhood involves both needing relationship and fearing the other who may threaten loss of relationship and that control, whether by means of coercion of the other or self-monitoring of behavior, is a response to that deep ambivalence. Bodies of victims will also signify ambivalence, perhaps acting one way in one moment and another in the next, or both wanting to be rid of pain and yet recognizing pain as a sign of being still alive, or feeling one way in her body even though her mind is saying something else.

21. Butler, *Bodies that Matter*, 241.
22. M. R. Mahoney, "Victimization or Oppression?"
23. Gondolf and Fisher, *Battered Women*.
24. M. R. Mahoney, "Victimization or Oppression?" 72–73.

Any disavowal of the multiple layers and interrelated factors that make a person who she is in the whole range of human experience reduces agency, and therefore lessens the possibility of resistance.

Well intentioned ministers of pastoral care may insist that the victim is not at fault or to blame but when victims claim some responsibility their claims must be taken seriously for what they are. In theological terms a person's acknowledgement of her or his own propensity to sin, to act for the diminishment of life rather than its enrichment, will lead to greater freedom, not less. Lamb argues "that the large majority of perpetrators had enough free will not to do what they did, and, more controversially, that more than a few victims also had enough free choice to make their self-blame, at times, reasonable."[25] This does not mean letting the perpetrator off the hook of responsibility and accountability; it does not mean blaming the victim; it does mean acknowledging that the victim is a participant in a multifaceted dynamic. Their participation is not equal and the assessment of that inequality is something that the pastoral care provider can bring to the situation, but this should not be built on a total rejection and denial of the victim's complicity.

The pastoral relationship with a victim will foster the agency needed for resistance inasmuch as power is used in that relationship mutually, not unilaterally. The minister of pastoral care can also open up awareness to the use of power in the relationship between victim and perpetrator, both through sharing of information and through the pastoral relationship itself. When used unilaterally the power of interrelatedness works to diminish the subjectivity of both parties and ultimately to destroy agency altogether. But to be alive is to exercise power for at least a minimal amount of subjectivity. When the ambiguity of relationship is split, rather than held in tension it is both the result of and the precipitating factor for unilateral use of power that seeks to control relationship in order to assure oneself of on-going survival. In the context of a relationship built on the full range of life, on giving and receiving, on loving and being loved, the splits can be reintegrated and more—more emotional and material resources, more of the power of the web, more of God—is then available for sustaining the paradoxes and tensions at the heart of life. Increased subjectivity and liberation are the results, not of clear conviction to one side or the other but of clear

---

25. Lamb, *Trouble with Blame*, 12.

conviction that ambiguity and ambivalence are inevitable to life itself and part of the fullness of God. Acts of resistance need not be based on unambivalent clarity but can simply be tentative acts of uncertainty in the hope of more life. The key is to act in the way that seems most likely to work for more life given what is known in the moment[26] and in spite of ambiguity, trusting that the next moment will be different and can provide different knowledge and possibilities. But how will the minister of pastoral care and the victim assess which is the more likely path to resistance rather than to further abuse? This question is taken up in the next section.

Pursuit of Contradictions and Exclusions

The way of resistance becomes apparent at the constitutive outside that delineates the inside in any categorization made by culture in the process of constructing subjectivity. Every iteration of a norm in word, action, symbol, etc. is an intentional process of identification for the purpose of upholding the status of the identification as normative. A pastoral care interested in resistance to the re-edification of norms deemed, by best assessment, to be life diminishing will pursue the exclusions assumed by the reiteration and the contradictions within various fields of culture. This means always questioning what is not said in addition to what is said, what is not being assumed along with the unspoken assumptions. Attention to the means by which categorical assumptions work to keep power used in a unilateral mode will open up possibilities for power to be used otherwise and will point to the means by which resistance may be enacted.

For victims of intimate partner violence, pursuit of contradictions means exploring in more detail what was revealed about oneself and the relational dynamic when the victim fought back, as in the earlier example from Rodriguez's story. That action is a contradiction to the norm. It may reveal a motivation to live, to be a better mother, to take control, or the ability to feel angry and it also may reveal the horror of what it means for someone to "whack" someone else. Pursuit of exclusions leads one to question the terms of identification and definition,

---

26. This should not be interpreted to minimize the risk of death in many cases of domestic violence but rather to point out that the path of resistance always involves risks and always involves some ambiguity.

asking, "whom does it serve?" Victims often work hard to try to define abuse because if what is happening to them is abuse, according to current standards, then anger or leaving might be justified. When the limits of the definition, the fine line between what counts and what doesn't count, are sought not only is the hegemonic construction that sustains the abuse of women revealed, but also the path for resistance. Rodriguez's statement that she mistook beatings for "impassioned" love means that at some point she must have looked at the way "passion" was defined and reinforced. She then considered that there was another possibility for that definition, or felt the contradiction within a culture, and her own body, of passion that is supposed to feel good and yet feels like pain. When the other possibilities are revealed or imagined the body and the psyche are changed in the very act of imagining something different.[27] Repression may open up and mapping, to use our earlier terms, may shift and change thus recreating a slightly new person with more of life available to her. That which was unthinkable is now thinkable and the disallowed may now be allowed.

The pursuit of contradictions and exclusions raises some crucial issues for the pastoral relationship. First, it means, given the victim's exclusion in the violent relationship, and in the broader culture, that to follow the victim's lead is to follow the path to resistance. The path to increased subjectivity and liberation is best known through those allowed the least subjectivity. Those whose bodies are ignored and discounted, those whose voices and actions have the least influence on others, are "our teachers," to use Soelle's terms. Pursuit of the margins of the culture/psyche/body enlarges the whole, enriches life, and reveals more of God. This is where the wisdom of God is most evident.

Another area for consideration in pastoral relationships is the way in which ministers of pastoral care and victims themselves construct the category "victim." With the heightened awareness of the widespread problem of abuse and its effects on victims, "victim" has, in many ways, become an identity category lacking in ambiguity. Battered women often resist being identified as such because it suggests that they are "helpless victims." To be a "victim" has come to mean that one has no responsibility for the situation that has victimized them, that one cannot also be a "perpetrator," that one must always be helped but not confronted or

---

27. Recall the discussion in chapter 4 of Scarry, *Body in Pain*.

held accountable. Lamb points out that while it was once important for the purpose of heightening public awareness to stress the harm done to individual women by abuse it is now used to pathologize (post trauma) victims and to test for the validity of their victimhood.[28] She states:

> In place of the victim-blaming that occurred decades ago, we —and by "we" I mean psychologists, researchers, therapists, feminists, victims' rights organizations, the media, activists, and survivor groups—have offered up for public discourse a different version of the victim that has its own problems. Here, the image of the victim is one who is pure, innocent, blameless, and free of problems (before the abuse). This version is often presented in juxtaposition with the perpetrator as evil monster.[29]

A pastoral care of resistance must attend to the exclusions made in attempts to categorize and identify victims. Intimate partner violence varies in degree; some abuse is more severe than others. Victims often do continue on with their lives without significant "damage" from the abuse. They do not necessarily develop personality disorders or other mental health or relational impairment. Ministers of pastoral care must ask themselves how their own category of "victim" is founded on what makes and does not make someone a victim and realize that the path of resistance may be found in their own acts of foreclosure. Likewise victims will also have to examine the exclusions they make in accepting and/or rejecting the identity of "victim," or pushing to maintain themselves as "agents" in the violence. What is assumed by that label? This contest over the categorization "victim" reveals one path to resistance as it becomes clear that the term coincides with the individualization and de-politicizing of intimate partner violence, which goes on to serve the reign of patriarchal gender hegemony.

Political Analysis and Advocacy

Agency is a "political prerogative." It is assigned according to the regulations of the culture for the benefit of those who are allowed to make the

---

28. There are many writers in the field of domestic violence who take up these issues, including Ferraro, "Dance of Dependency;" Lamb, *New Visions of Victims*; M. R. Mahoney, "Victimization or Oppression?" Schneider, "Particularity and Generality." These include critiques of the criminalization of domestic violence, the recovery movement, and Post-traumatic stress diagnosis.

29. Lamb, "Constructing the Victim," 108.

regulations. A pastoral care of resistance will engage in political analysis and advocacy because however aware of it any individual pastoral caregiver might be, pastoral care is always a political act.[30] The question that must be asked, as Soelle reminds us, is whom does our pastoral care serve? Will it serve those persons and ideologies using power for the coercion of others, or will it serve to enrich the web with relationships of mutuality in subversion of existing modes of oppression?

In the context of intimate partner violence political analysis can help address the problems posed above. When domestic violence is understood from the perspective of its root in patriarchal culture the "ordinariness" of abuse problematizes the individualization that occurs in the criminal justice and mental health systems. As Martha Mahoney states:

> The fiction that violence is exceptional is fundamental to stereotypes that portray battered women as helpless, dependent, and pathological. If it were understood that violence is really everywhere, then it would not be difficult to accept that violence happens to ordinary women. Individual women could then begin to overcome their own denial of painful experiences, a particularly dangerous component of broader social denial of the prevalence and seriousness of domestic violence.[31]

It is the political analysis of intimate partner violence as a logical eventuality of patriarchal ideologies and practices that helps individual women understand themselves as both victims of perpetrators and oppression *and* as agents of their lives and active participants in the world. The yielding of the power and dominance critique to "symptomatology"[32] has thwarted efforts to ameliorate suffering and increase subjectivity and liberation. When, as Lambs says, "the primary methods of dealing with abuse became individual therapy and individual redress through the law and the police, the political became personal; generalized culture became personalized culture."[33] This shift to the personal severed from the political has worked to obfuscate the political dynamics at play and ultimately works to sustain the violence. As Lamb goes on to point

---

30. Others in pastoral theology and care have also made this claim. See, for instance, Pattison, *Critique of Pastoral Care*, and *Pastoral Care and Liberation Theology*.
31. M. R. Mahoney, "Victimization or Oppression?" 59–92.
32. Lamb, *New Visions of Victims*, 110.
33. Ibid., 131.

out, "Talking about the world of women and the expectation of violence in the lives of women moves away from creating a separate category of 'victim' that a mental health condition can nicely explain. Instead, it moves to a political stance: that the girl is a victim of something endemic in our culture—male violence."[34]

There are victims and there are perpetrators; both act but the extent to which each can act in resistance varies according to the political regulations for what it means to be subject, male/female, wife/husband, married/partnered, dependent/independent, making love/making war. The extent to which one "has" agency is linked to the extent to which an act of the subject is recognized. The terms of "choice" to act or not act in particular ways are set by political structures and ideologies that determine what choices are allowed, how they will be received, the costs and benefits at stake, and even which choices are conceivable. It is political analysis that will articulate why it is that batterers are more able to resist the culture they are made of than are their victims and thus can be held more responsible and accountable for their actions. If, to quote Lamb once again, "the problem were viewed from a more political stance, it would be that women can't go through life expecting not to be abused without some change in society. We would then take action to change perpetrators and change men, starting with the development of boys."[35] This is a call for a broader understanding of victimization, one that is more inclusive of the multiple and interrelated factors involved and one that requires action.

A pastoral care for resistance requires advocacy for the change of political practices and discourses that perpetuate suffering. It requires assessment of relative position in the web of culture and of the ways in which power is used. Agency is always a political struggle wherein some have more and some have less. In order to increase subjectivity for victims and thus enrich the web of life for all of us, ministers of pastoral care will need to engage not only in a sociopolitical outlook but in subversive acts of resistance that challenge the prevailing reign of violence. In that sense God requires of us a "fighting spirit," as Soelle calls it, an unquenchable yearning and active pursuit of the more abundant life that is possible for all of us.

34. Ibid., 133.
35. Ibid., 134.

Summary

The thesis for this book stated that there is a way to theologically conceptualize human personhood as deeply constructed in and constituted of culture, both as psyche and body, and identify human agency as arising ambiguously from that very process of construction. I have attempted to take seriously the work of pastoral care with and for victims of intimate partner violence in proposing one way of thinking about human personhood. I have theologically grounded this proposal in the notion of an ontological dynamic interrelatedness that can be identified as God. It has been my hope to construct theological language that will make sense in light of efforts to increase the subjectivity of victims through an understanding of the inextricability of human and divine. Agency is a crucial issue in the dynamic of intimate partner violence as we contemplate how the suffering involved in this violence might be stopped. Who can stop it and how? Resistance to the culture of violence requires agency, a capacity to act and have an effect. I have tried to suggest a way in which we can understand persons as both subject to cultural norms and able to resist those norms, not from a place outside of culture but by turning the power of cultural construction upon itself. The ambiguous nature of human and divine agency points, however, to a deep ambivalence in life and thus in any contemplation or activity of resistance.

I opened with questions about how one can be a victim of oppression, and so deeply formed by that victimization, and an agent of resistance at the same time. I asked to what extent ministers of pastoral care can hold persons responsible for change, to what extent is their life determined by external factors and what can be attributed to internal factors? In response to those questions I have proposed a reorienting of how the internal and the external are conceived. Victims direct us to the path for healing, liberation, and more life. They suggest to us that pastoral care must be framed in terms of its capacity to resist meaningless suffering. I am suggesting four ways that ministers of pastoral care might do this: by encouraging attachment to the now and to more life, by acknowledging and accepting ambiguity, by pursuing contradictions and exclusions, and by engaging in political analysis and advocacy. These are sure to be "impure" suggestions, certainly working for complicity, but hopefully also for at least a bit of resistance. They will, I expect, be challenged, unsettled and deconstructed and in the process it is my hope that a better future might be forged in spite of our limited understating of what "better" can be.

Bibliography

Ackerman, Denise M., and Riet Bons-Storm, editors. *Liberating Faith Practices: Feminist Practical Theologies and Context*. Leuven: Peeters, 1998.
Adams, Carol J. *Woman-Battering*. Creative pastoral Care and Counseling Series. Minneapolis: Fortress, 1994.
Alcoff, Linda. "Cultural Feminism Versus Post-Structuralism: The Identity Crisis in Feminist Theory." *Signs* 13 (1988) 405–36.
Ali, Carroll A. Watkins. *Survival and Liberation: Pastoral Theology in African American Context*. St. Louis: Chalice, 1999.
Benjamin, Jessica. *The Bonds of Love: Psychoanalysis, Feminism, and the Problem of Domination*. New York: Pantheon, 1988.
———. *Like Subjects, Love Objects: Essays on Recognition and Sexual Difference*. New Haven: Yale University Press, 1995.
———. *Shadow of the Other: Intersubjectivity and Gender in Psychoanalysis*. New York: Routledge, 1998.
Bettenhausen, Elizabeth. "Free Will." In *Dictionary of Feminist Theologies*, edited by Letty Russell and J. Shannon Clarkson. Louisville: Westminster John Knox, 1996.
Bons-Storm, Riet. *The Incredible Woman: Listening to Women's Silences in Pastoral Care and Counseling*. Nashville: Abingdon, 1996.
Bordo, Susan. *Unbearable Weight: Feminism, Western Culture, and the Body*. Berkeley: University of California Press, 1987.
Bourdieu, Pierre. *In Other Words: Essays Towards a Reflexive Sociology*. Translated by Matthew Adamson. Cambridge: Polity, 1990.
———. *The Logic of Practice*. Translated by Richard Nice. Stanford: Stanford University Press, 1990.
———, and Loïc J. D. Wacquant. *An Invitation to Reflexive Sociology*. Chicago: University of Chicago, 1992.
Browne, Angela. *When Battered Women Kill*. New York: Free Press, 1987.
Browning, Don S. *Religious Thought and the Modern Psychologies: A Critical Conversation in the Theology of Culture*. Philadelphia: Fortress, 1987.
Butler, Judith. *Gender Trouble: Feminism and the Subversion of Identity*. New York: Routledge, 1990.
———. "Contingent Foundations." In *Feminists Theorize the Political*, edited by Judith Butler and Joan Scott, 3–21. New York: Routledge, 1992.
———. *Bodies That Matter: On the Discursive Limits of "Sex."* New York: Routledge, 1993.
———. *The Psychic Life of Power: Theories in Subjection*. Stanford: Stanford University Press, 1997.

———, and Joan Scott, editors. *Feminists Theorize the Political*. New York: Routledge, 1992.

Celani, David. *The Illusion of Love: Why the Battered Woman Returns to Her Abuser*. New York: Columbia University Press, 1994.

Clarke, Paul Barry. "Free Will." In *Dictionary of Ethics, Theology and Society*, edited by Paul Barry Clarke and Andrew Linzey, 381–88. London: Routledge, 1996.

Clarke, Rita-Lou. *Pastoral Care of Battered Women*. Philadelphia: Westminster, 1986.

Clemetson, Lynette. "Oprah at a Crossroads." *Newsweek*, January 8, 2001, 38–47.

Cooey, Paula. "Re-Membering the Body: A Theological Resource for Resisting Domestic Violence." *Theology and Sexuality* 3 (1995) 27–47.

———. *Religious Imagination and the Body: A Feminist Analysis*. New York: Oxford University Press, 1994.

Cooper-White, Pamela. *The Cry of Tamar: Violence against Women and the Church's Response*. Minneapolis: Fortress, 1995.

———. "An Emperor without Clothes: The Church's Views about Treatment of Domestic Violence." *Pastoral Psychology* 45 (1996) 3–20.

Dean, William. "Deconstruction and Process Theology." *Journal of Religion* 64 (1992) 1–19.

Dobash, R. Emerson, and Russell Dobash. *Violence against Wives: A Case against the Patriarchy*. New York: Free, 1979.

Doehring, Carrie. "A Method of Feminist Pastoral Theology." In *Feminist and Womanist Pastoral Theology*, edited by Bonnie J. Miller-McLemore and Brita L. Gill-Austern, 95–112. Nashville: Abingdon, 1999.

———. *Taking Care: Monitoring Power Dynamics and Relational Boundaries in Pastoral Care and Counseling*. Nashville: Abingdon, 1995.

Dunlap, Susan. "Discourse Theory and Pastoral Theology." In *Feminist and Womanist Pastoral Theology*, edited by Bonnie J. Miller-McLemore and Brita L. Gill-Austern, 133–48. Nashville: Abingdon, 1999.

Eugene, Toinette M., and James Newton Poling. *Balm for Gilead: Pastoral Care for African American Families Experiencing Abuse*. Nashville: Abingdon, 1998.

Fairbairn, W. R. D. *Psychoanalytic Studies of the Personality*. London: Routledge and Kegan Paul, 1952.

———. "Libido Theory Re-Evaluated." In *From Instinct to Self: Selected Papers of W. R. D. Fairburn*, edited by David E. Scharff and Elinor Fairbairn Birtles, 2:115–56. Northvale, NJ: Aronson, 1930.

———. "ExperimentalND Aspects of Psychoanalysis." In *From Instinct to Self: Selected Papers of W. R. D. Fairburn*, edited by David E Scharff and Ellinor Fairbairn Birtles, 1:103–110. Northvale, NJ: Aronson, 1952.

———. "In Defence of Object Relations Theory." In *From Instinct to Self: Selected Papers of W. R. D. Fairburn*, edited by David E. Scharff and Ellinor Fairbairn Birtles, 1:111–28. Northvale, NJ: Aronson, 1955.

———. "The Nature of Hysterical States." In *From Instinct to Self: Selected Papers of W. R. D. Fairbairn*, edited by David E. Scharff and Ellinor Fairbairn Birtles, 1:13–40. Northvale, NJ: Aronson, 1954.

———. "On the Nature and Aims of Psychoanalytical Treatment." In *From Instinct to Self: Selected Papers of W. R. D. Fairburn*, edited by David E. Scharff and Elinor Fairbairn Birtles, 1:74–92. Northvale, NJ: Aronson, 1958.

———. "Replies to 'Reevaluating Concepts.'" In *From Instinct to Self: Selected Papers of W. R. D. Fairburn*, edited by David E. Scharff and Elinor Fairbairn Birtles, 1:149–54. Northvale, NJ: Aronson, 1994.

Ferraro, Kathleen. "The Dance of Dependency: A Genealogy of Domestic Violence Discourse." *Hypatia* 11 (1996) 77–91.

Flax, Jane. *Thinking Fragments: Psychoanalysis, Feminism, and Postmodernism in the Conteporary West*. Berkeley: University of California Press, 1990.

———. *Disputed Subjects: Essays on Psychoanalysis, Politics and Philosophy*. New York: Routledge, 1993.

Fortune, Marie. *Violence in the Family: A Workshop Curriculum for Clergy and Other Helpers*. Cleveland: Pilgrim, 1989.

Fraser, Nancy. "The Uses and Abuses of French Discourse Theories for Feminist Politics." In *Revaluing French Feminism: Critical Essays on Difference, Agency and Culture*, edited by Nancy Fraser and Sandra Lee Bartky, 177–94. Bloomington: Indiana University Press, 1992.

Fraser, Nancy, and Sandra Lee Bartky, editors. *Revaluing French Feminism: Critical Essays on Difference, Agency, and Culture*. Bloomington: Indiana University Press, 1992.

Gelles, Richard J., and Murray A. Straus. *Intimate Violence*. New York: Simon and Schuster, 1988.

Glaz, Maxine, and Jeanne Stevenson Moessner, editors. *Women in Travail and Transition*. Minneapolis: Fortress, 1991.

Gondolf, Edward. *Batterer Intervention Systems: Issues, Outcomes, and Recommendations*. Thousand Oaks, CA: Sage, 2002.

———, and Ellen Fisher. *Battered Women as Survivors: An Alternative to Treating Learned Helplessness*. Lexington, MA: Lexington, 1988.

Gordon, Linda. *Heroes of Their Own Lives: The Politcs and History of Family Violence in America*. New York: Viking, 1988.

Graham, Elaine. *Making the Difference: Gender, Pershonhood and Theology*. Minneapolis: Fortress, 1996.

———. *Transforming Practice: Pastoral Theology in an Age of Uncertainty*. London: Mowbray, 1996.

Graham, Larry. *Care of Persons, Care of Worlds: A Psychosystems Approach to Pastoral Care and Counseling*. Nashville: Abingdon, 1992.

Greenberg, Jay R., and Stephen A. Mitchell. *Object Relations in Psychoanalytic Theory*. Cambridge: Harvard University Press, 1983.

Hartsock, Nancy. "Foucault on Power: A Theory for Women?" In *Feminism/Postmodernism*, edited by Linda Nicholson, 157–75. New York: Routledge, 1992.

Hekman, Susan. "Subjects and Agents: The Question for Feminism." In *Provoking Agents: Gender and Agency in Theory and Practice*, edited by Judith Kegan Gardiner, 194–207. Urbana: University of Illinois Press, 1995.

Herman, Judith. *Trauma and Recovery: The Aftermath of Violence—from Domestic Abuse to Political Terror*. New York: Basic, 1992.

Hiltner, Seward. *Preface to Pastoral Theology*. New York: Abingdon, 1958.

Hirschmann, Nancy J. "The Theory and Practice of Freedom: The Case of Battered Women." In *Reconstructing Political Theory: Feminist Perspectives*, edited by Mary

Lyndon Shanley and Uma Narayan, 194–210. University Park: Pennsylvania State University Press, 1997.

Jaggar, Alison, and Susan Bordo, editors. *Gender/Body/Knowledge: Feminist Reconstructions of Being and Knowing*. New Brunswick: Rutgers University Press, 1989.

Jones, Ann. *Next Time, She'll Be Dead: Battering and How to Stop It*. Boston: Beacon, 1994.

Jones, Kathleen. *Living between Danger and Love: The Limits of Choice*. New Brunswick: Rutgers University Press, 2000.

Jones, Serene. *Feminist Theory and Christian Theology: Cartographies of Grace*. Minneapolis: Fortress, 2000.

Jordan, Judith, Alexandra G. Kaplan, Jean Baker Miller, Irene Stiver, and Janet Surrey, editors. *Women's Growth in Connection: Writings from the Stone Center*. New York: Guilford, 1991.

Lamb, Sharon. "Constructing the Victim: Popular Images and Lasting Labels." In *New Versions of Victims*, edited by Sharon Lamb, 108–38. New York: New York University Press, 1999.

———. *The Trouble with Blame: Victims, Perpetrators, and Responsibility*. Cambridge,: Harvard University Press, 1996.

———, editor. *New Visions of Victims: Feminists Struggle with the Concept*. New York: New York University Press, 1999.

Lobel, Kerry, editor. *Naming the Violence: Speaking Out about Lesbian Battering*. Seattle: Seal, 1986.

Loomer, Bernard. "A Process-Relational Conception of Creation." In *Cry of the Environment*, edited by Phillip Jornason and Ken Butigan. Santa Fe: Bear, 1984.

———. "Dimensions of Freedom." In *Bernard Lee*, edited by Harry James Cargas, 323–40. New York: Paulist, 1976.

———. "The Free and Relational Self." In *Belief and Ethics: Essays in Ethics, the Human Sciences, and Ministry in Honor of W. Alvin Pitcher*, edited by W. Widick Schroeder and Gibson Winter. Chicago: Center for the Scientific Study of Religion, 1978.

———. "On Committing Yourself to a Relationship." *Process Studies* 16 (1987) 255–63.

———. "S-I-Z-E." *Criterion* 13 (1974) 5–8.

———. "The Size of God." In *The Size of God: The Theology of Bernard Loomer in Context*, edited by William Dean and Larry Axel. Macon: Mercer University Press, 1987.

———. "Theology in the American Grain." In *Process Philosophy and Social Thought*, edited by John B. Cobb Jr. and W. Widick Schroeder. Chicago: Center for the Scientific Study of Religion, 1981.

———. "Two Conceptions of Power." *Process Studies* 6 (1976) 5–32.

———. *Unfoldings: Conversations from the Morning Seminars of Bernie Loomer*. Berkeley: First Unitarian Church Berkeley, 1985.

Lorde, Audre. "The Master's Tools Will Never Dismantle the Master's House." In *Sister Outsider*, by Audre Lorde, 110–13. Freedom, CA: Crossing, 1984.

Mahoney, Martha R. "Victimization or Oppression? Women's Lives, Violence, and Agency." In *The Public Nature of Private Violence*, edited by Martha A. Fineman and Roxanne Mykitiuk, 59–92. New York: Routledge, 1994.

Mahoney, Maureen, and Barbara Yngvesson. "The Construction of Subjectivity and the Paradox of Resistance: Reintegrating Feminist Anthropology and Psychology." *Signs* 18 (1992) 44.

McFague, Sallie. *The Body of God: An Ecological Theology*. Minneapolis: Fortress, 1993.

Meyers, Diana. "Agency." In *A Companion to Feminist Philosophy*, edited by Alison Jaggar. Cambridge: Blackwell, 1998.

———. *Subjection and Subjectivity: Psychoanalytic Feminism and Moral Philosophy*. New York: Routledge, 1994.

Miller, Jean Baker. *Toward a New Psychology of Women*. Boston: Beacon, 1976.

———, and Irene P. Stiver. *The Healing Connection: How Women Form Relationships in Therapy and Life*. Boston: Beacon, 1997.

Miller-McLemore, Bonnie. "The Subject and Practice of Pastoral Theology as a Practical Theological Discipline: Pushing Past the Nagging Identity Crisis to the Poetics of Resistance." In *Liberating Faith Practices: Feminist Pracitical Theologies and Context*, edited by Denise M. Ackerman and Riet Bons-Storm, 175–98. Leuven: Peeters, 1998.

———. "Feminist Theory in Pastoral Theology." In *Feminist and Womanist Pastoral Theology*, edited by Bonnie J. Miller-McLemore and Brita L. Gill-Austern, 77–94. Nashville: Abingdon, 1999.

———. "The Living Human Web: Pastoral Theology at the Turn of the Century." In *Through the Eyes of Women: Insights for Pastoral Care*, edited by Jeanne Stevenson Moessner, 9–26. Philadelphia: Westminster John Knox, 1996.

———, and Brita L. Gill-Austern, editors. *Feminist and Womanist Pastoral Theology*. Nashville: Abingdon, 1999.

Mills, Linda G. *Insult to Injury: Rethinking Our Responses to Intimate Abuse*. Princeton: Princeton University Press, 2003.

Mitchell, Stephen A. *Relational Concepts in Psychoanalysis: An Integration*. Cambridge: Harvard University Press, 1988.

———. "True Selves, False Selves, and the Ambiguity of Authenticity." In *Relational Perspectives in Psychoanalysis*, edited by Neil J. Skolnick and Susan C. Warshaw, 1–20. Hillsdale, NJ: Analytic, 1992.

———, and Lewis Aron, editors. *Relational Psychoanalysis: The Emergence of a Tradition*. Hillsdale, NJ: Analytic, 1999.

Moessner, Jeanne Stevenson, editor. *Through the Eyes of Women: Insights for Pastoral Care*. Philadelphia: Westminster John Knox, 1996.

Moraga, Cherie, and Gloria Anzaldua, editors. *This Bridge Called my Back: Writings by Radical Women of Color*. New York: Kitchen Table, 1983.

Nason-Clark, Nancy. *The Battered Wife: How Christians Confront Family Violence*. Louisville: Westminster John Knox, 1997.

Neuger, Christie Cozad. *Counseling Women: A Narrative, Pastoral Approach*. Minneapolis: Fortress, 2001.

———. "Feminist Pastoral Theology and Pastoral Counseling: A Work in Progress." *Journal of Pastoral Theology* 2 (1992) 35–57.

———. "A Feminist Perspective on Pastoral Counseling with Women." In *Clinical Handbook of Pastoral Counseling* Volume 3, edited by Robert J. Wicks and Richard D. Parsons, 17–37. Mahwah: Paulist, 1993.

———, editor. *The Arts of Ministry: Feminist-Womanist Approaches*. Lousiville: Westminster John Knox, 1996.

———. "Pastoral Counseling as an Art of Personal Political Activism." In *The Arts of Ministry: Feminist-Womanist Approaches*, edited by Christie Cozad Neuger, 88–117. Lousiville: Westminster John Knox, 1996.

Norwood, Robin. *Women Who Love Too Much*. Los Angeles: Tarcher, 1985.

Pattison, Stephen. *A Critique of Pastoral Care*. London: SCM, 1993.

———. *Pastoral Care and Liberation Theology*. Cambridge: Cambridge University Press, 1994.

Poling, James. *The Abuse of Power: A Theological Problem*. Nashville: Abingdon, 1991.

Ramsay, Nancy. "Compassionate Resistance: An Ethic for Pastoral Care and Counseling." *Journal of Pastoral Care* 52 (1998) 217–26.

Renzetti, Claire. *Violent Betrayal*. New York: Sage, 1992.

———. "The Challenge to Feminism Posed by Women's Use of Violence in Intimate Relationships." In *New Versions of Victims: Feminists Struggle with the Concept*, edited by Sharon Lamb, 42–56. New York: New York University Press, 1999.

Rodriguez, Stephanie. *Time to Stop Pretending*. Middlebury, VT: Eriksson, 1994.

Ryan, Maura. "Agency." In *Dictionary of Feminist Theologies*, edited by Letty Russell and J. Shannon Clarkson, 4–5. Louisville: Westminster John Knox, 1996.

Scarry, Elaine. *The Body in Pain: The Making and Unmaking of the World*. New York: Oxford University Press, 1985.

Scharff, David E., and Ellinor Fairbairn Birtles, editors. *From Instinct to Self: Selected Papers of W. R. D. Fairbairn*. 2 vols. Northvale, NJ: Aronson, 1994.

Schecter, Susan. *Women and Male Violence: The Visions and Struggles of the Battered Women's Movement*. Boston: South End, 1982.

Schneider, Elizabeth. "Particularity and Generality: Challenges of Feminist Theory and Practice in Work on Women-Abuse." *New York Univeristy Law Review* 67 (1992) 520–68.

Skolnick, Neil, and David Scharff, editors. *Fairbarin, Then and Now*. Hillsdale, NJ: Analytic, 1998.

Soelle, Dorothee. *Choosing Life*. Translated by Margaret Kohl. Philadelphia: Fortress, 1981.

———. *Creative Disobedience*. Translated by Lawrence W. Denef. Cleveland: Pilgrim, 1995.

———. *The Silent Cry: Mysticism and Resistance*. Translated by Barbara and Martin Rumscheidt. Minneapolis: Fortress, 2001.

———. *The Strength of the Weak: Toward a Christian Feminist Identity*. Translated by Robert and Rita Kimber. Philadelphia: Westminster, 1984.

———. *Suffering*. Translated by Everett Kalin. Philadelphia: Fortress, 1975.

———. *Theology for Skeptics: Reflections on God*. Translated by Joyce L. Irwin. Minneapolis: Fortress, 1995.

———. *Thinking About God: An Introduction to Theology*. Translated by John Bowden. London: SCM, 1990.

———, with Shirley Cloyes. *To Work and to Love: A Theology of Creation*. Philadelphia: Fortress, 1984.
Spelman, Elizabeth. *Inessential Woman: Problems of Exclusion in Feminist Thought*. Boston: Beacon, 1988.
Stark, Evan, and Anne Flitcraft. *Women at Risk: Domestic Violence and Women's Health*. Thousand Oaks, CA: Sage, 1996.
Sutherland, J. D. *Fairbairn's Journey into the Interior*. London: Free Association, 1989.
Suchocki, Marjorie. "Radical Empiricism: Radical Enough?" *American Journal of Theology and Philosophy* 13 (1992) 171–81.
Walker, Gillian. *Family Violence and the Women's Movement*. Toronto: University of Toronto Press, 1990.
Walker, Lenore E. *The Battered Woman*. New York: Harper & Row, 1979.
———. *The Battered Woman Syndrome*. Focus on Women 6. New York: Springer, 1984.
Weedon, Chris. *Feminist Practice and Poststructuralist Theory*. 2nd ed. Oxford: Blackwell, 1997.
White, Evelyn. *Chain, Chain, Change: For Black Women Dealing with Physical and Emotional Abuse*. Seattle: Seal, 1985.
Whitehead, Alfred North. *The Function of Reason*. Boston: Beacon, 1958.
———. *Modes of Thought*. New York: Macmillan, 1933.
———. *Process and Reality: An Essay in Cosmology*. Corrected ed. Edited by David Ray Griffin and Donald W. Sherburne. New York: Free Press, 1978.

www.ingramcontent.com/pod-product-compliance
Lightning Source LLC
Chambersburg PA
CBHW062046220426
43662CB00010B/1679